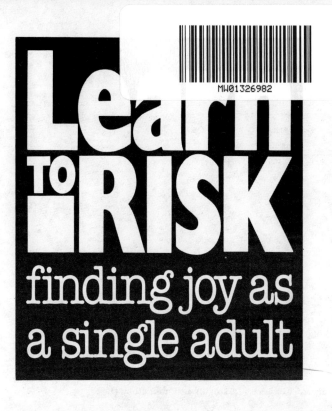

Learn to Risk
finding joy as a single adult

BOBBIE REED, Ph.D.

PYRANEE BOOKS

Zondervan Publishing House
Grand Rapids, Michigan

LEARN TO RISK
Copyright © 1990 by Bobbie Reed

Pyranee Books is an imprint of Zondervan Publishing House, 1415 Lake Drive, S.E., Grand Rapids, Michigan 49506.

Library of Congress Cataloging-in-Publication Data

Reed, Bobbie
    Learn to risk : finding joy as a single adult / Bobbie Reed.
      p. cm.
    Includes bibliographical references.
    ISBN 0-310-28711-1
    1. Single. 2. Single people—Religious life. 3. Self-
  actualization (Psychology) I. Title.
  HQ800.R4   1990   89−24290
                                                                                                                        CIP

Unless otherwise noted, all Scripture references are taken from the *Holy Bible: New International Version* (North American Edition), copyright © 1973, 1978, 1984 by the International Bible Society. Used by permission of Zondervan Bible Publishers.

All rights reserved. No part of this publication may be reproduced, stored in a retrieval system, or transmitted in any form or by any means—electronic, mechanical, photocopy, recording, or any other—except for brief quotations in printed reviews, without the prior permission of the publisher.

Printed in the United States of America

90 91 92 93 94 95 96 / PP / 10 9 8 7 6 5 4 3 2 1

*To Sylvia Porter,
a special woman
and a true friend,
with love.*

Contents

Introduction	7
1. Release the Fantasies	11
2. Live Beyond Rejection	25
3. Let Go of the Past	46
4. Forgive the Pain	58
5. Win Over Fear	72
6. Don't Wait for the "Wonderful"	84
7. Lern to Be Open, Honest, and Caring	100
8. Risk Reaching Out	119
9. Discover Joy	130
10. Celebrate Life	145
Notes	157

Introduction

"When I look ahead, sometimes I don't think I can face another day," Peggy confesses. "But when I look back to where I started from, I can't believe how far I've come!" she admits with a smile.

"Most of the time I'm happy as a single who's never been married," Sheila shares, "but there are times when I really wish my prince would come along and whisk me away."

"I didn't enjoy myself much as a single the first time," Trent admits warily. "Now that I'm single again, I hate it!"

This book is for single adults—those who have always been single or who are single again either from death of a spouse or divorce. Life is often tough, and the road seems full of unexpected potholes and unwelcome detours. Wanting to avoid such problems, all of us tend to find a comfortable rut to travel in, but we end up stuck in that rut. The principles provided here offer a way to find hope and joy in otherwise tough situations for single people.

So let's break out of stuck places and get on with the abundant life God wishes for us.[1] To unstick ourselves, we must realize that the abundant life is not a prescribed set of circumstances God sets up for us, a fulfillment of all our dreams and hopes. Rather the abundant life is an attitude of expectancy, appreciation, and confidence that God will enable us to handle all of life's circumstances, even those that may look like nightmares. The abundant life is ours for the choosing. That's the key word—*choosing*. God will never force his ways on us. We must choose them. And that's what this book can help you do: recognize the rut you may be traveling in and encourage you to choose God's ways.

One of the common ruts we may choose is living in a fantasy world. We want life to imitate the happy unreality of fairy tales, movies, and novels. We pray that God will make our fantasies come true and sometimes get angry and feel he doesn't love us when he doesn't make the fairy-tale endings happen for us. While it may be okay to indulge in an occasional daydream, if we are to live fully, we must abandon our fantasies and face reality with courage and faith.

Sometimes we encounter one of life's harsher realities: rejection. Most of us have experienced a painful rejection at least once in our lives. Most of us have learned to regroup and rebuild. But some people seem to be stuck forever, afraid of ever reaching out again. They are imprisoned by their past. Only when we recognize the rut for what it is and dare to live again, can we once again move forward.

One of the first steps to getting unstuck is to let go of the past, whether that involves a rejection experience, a personal failure, an embarrassment, or a lost dream. We need to follow the apostle Paul's example: let go of the past and press on to what God has prepared for us.[2] The exciting truth is that when we choose to let go of the past, we create space in our lives for God to fill with something (someone?) new and exciting!

Usually before we can totally let go of our past, we must learn to forgive whoever or whatever has caused the pain that has been stunting our personal and spiritual growth. Forgiving is not easy. It costs a lot. But if the cost of forgiving is high, the cost of not forgiving is even higher!

Another rut that can keep us from growing is worry. We worry not only about what happens to us but also about what doesn't happen. If we're not careful, we can become so concerned that we become afraid to take any action. We become immobilized by fear! When we recognize this rut, we can choose to win over worry by trusting our lives to God's loving care.

Sometimes we get stuck in a rut because we wait around for something wonderful to happen to us. In the process of

INTRODUCTION

waiting, we miss a lot of opportunities to meet new people, to try new activities, to get involved in new ministries, or to enjoy life! We don't need to sit passively and watch life pass us by. We can choose to take steps toward becoming the persons God has given us the potential to be.

As we break free of our ruts, we can learn to become more open, honest, and caring in our relationships. Before we can expect our friends to be open and caring with us, we must learn how to sow these qualities in our relationships, basing our actions on the principle that we reap what we sow.

As we grow in relational skills, we'll find that our relationships will deepen and become more intimate. Our need for intimacy will motivate us to risk reaching out to make new friends.

Growth in our abilities to love and care for others will result in new joy in our lives. If certain things block our joy, we can choose to remove those joy blockers. Christ promises that when we learn to abide in him, he will make our joy full.

And when our joy is full, we've moved out of our ruts and are prepared to celebrate life, to live each day with a sense of expectancy, to say with the psalmist David, "This is the day the Lord has made; let us rejoice and be glad in it."[3]

I'm aware of ruts and pain because I, too, have been single and then single again. After a ten-year marriage, I was divorced and spent two years as a single parent. I remember the days when I longed for fantasy rescuers to come along and solve my problems or the days when I dreamed of love, fearing I would never be loved again. But as I began to heal, to grow and to stretch, I found new joy waiting for me. Now for the past fifteen years, I have been active as a consultant for single adult ministries, as a counselor, and as a speaker for conferences. Each weekend I meet singles and listen to their stories. Some are stuck in ruts; some are growing.

My goal in this book is to encourage you, to cheer you on as you break out of your rut and learn to risk. In the following chapters you'll meet many single people: some in their ruts, others breaking free. I hope they both encourage and challenge you in your own journey as you learn to risk.

I also hope you'll involve yourself seriously in the activities listed at the end of each chapter. These activities are the practical, nuts-and-bolts part of the book. They are the tools that can help you explore and practice new ways of thinking and behaving.

The first set of activities is a self-assessment that will help you determine how you handle the issues covered in each chapter. Use these activities to explore your strengths and weaknesses, your healthy and unhealthy responses. Then follow the steps to begin to break out of your ruts.

The second set of activities is best done in a group. If you already have a support group—a singles' group, for instance—suggest that your group do some of these activities together; they may even want to discuss the whole book as a group. If you don't have a formal support group, consider finding one. Either find and join an existing group or build an informal one of your own. You can form a support group from people who love you—friends at work or in your church, family members who are especially sensitive, other single people who have similar experiences. Then as you work through this book, ask one or more of them to do some of the group activities with you, helping you not only to sort through the thought and behavior patterns that have gotten you stuck but also to encourage you as you learn to risk and grow.

1
Release the Fantasies

Dee Anne tapped her foot impatiently as she looked around the reception hall. Where was Dan, her husband of just a few minutes? He had muttered something about making her a queen and then had vanished, leaving her standing in the middle of the room, looking a bit forlorn in spite of the beautiful wedding gown billowing out around her. That had been almost forty-five minutes ago, Dee Anne noted, looking at her watch. Where was he?

Just as she was starting to become angry, the best man led her outside to the street. The entire wedding party and guests followed her. There, riding down the street on a horse, was a knight in a full set of shining armor. A trumpet sounded theatrically, startling the horse, who unexpectedly broke into a gallop, stopping only inches away from Dee Anne. Dan lumbered down awkwardly. The best man pulled out a ladder he had hidden earlier, and the newlyweds mounted the horse and rode off down the street, amid the laughter and cheers of their guests.[1]

A fantasy reenacted.

The office was abuzz. Gerry's parents had just won the Publisher's Clearing House Sweepstakes, and no one could believe it. "It's true," Gerry affirmed. "They won $100,000! I used to think that real people didn't win those things—that if anyone did, it was somehow fixed! But it happened. It really did!"

A fantasy come true.

I sat on the deck of a two-million-dollar home perched on top of a mountain, overlooking the ocean at the north end of Malibu. The owner of the home sat a few feet away, watching the pleasure on my face as I took in the view for the first time. He was a well-known author I had admired for years, and I couldn't believe we had finally met. Just as I was wondering what I was doing in such a place, he leaned forward and said, "Bobbie, what is your fantasy about this visit? I want to do everything I can to make it come true!"

A fantasy offered.

Carl mentally reviewed his resumé for the fifth time as he sat in the outer office, waiting to be interviewed by the company president. Carl had made the first and second cuts and was one of the top three applicants for the job. It was a dream job! The pay was nearly double his current salary. He would have a company car, an expense account, opportunity to travel to exotic places, and stock options in the company. His experience and expertise were perfectly suited to the job requirements. He wanted the job so badly he could hardly stand it! He prayed, not for the first time, "Please God, please!"

A fantasy desired.

DREAMERS ALL

Most of us have secret fantasies that we dream about and even pray about. Fantasies so wonderful, so incredible, so out of our reach that all we can do is hope that someday one of them might come true. We get our fantasies from many sources: novels, fairy tales, movies, television commercials, and even from the Bible. We read the real-life experiences of certain Bible characters and wish God would work the same miracles in our own lives.

Sally has an *Abigail fantasy*. Remember Abigail? Her story is told in the Old Testament.² She was the intelligent, beautiful, and brave wife of Nabal, a stubborn sheepherder with whom King David quarreled. Shortly after Nabal died, David sent Abigail a proposal of marriage. She accepted eagerly.

Sally, also a widow, is weary of waiting for a proposal and tired of being alone. She fantasizes about a famous person hearing of her and sending her a mysterious summons and a proposal of marriage.

Anna has a *Ruth fantasy*.³ When Ruth found the man she wanted to marry, she let him know of her interest, and he immediately took action to arrange for the wedding.

Things aren't that easy these days, Anna has found. But she keeps on trying. When Anna meets a new man who seems interesting, she asks him right out if he is ready for a committed relationship that could lead to marriage! She has scared away more than a few men.

Some single people have an *Adam fantasy*. You know the story of Adam.⁴ One day God looked down and said something like, "Oh, no! Adam, you're single! This won't do. Tell you what. You go to sleep, and I'll take care of it!" So God put Adam to sleep, extracted a rib, fashioned a woman, woke Adam, and brought Eve to him.

Singles with an Adam fantasy spend a lot of time alone, hiding out, sleeping, waiting as it were for God to perform a surgical miracle again and bring them the perfect mate. They don't often take the time to develop the relational skills that will help them meet and make friends with people of the opposite sex.

Still others have a *Rebekah fantasy*.⁵ Rebekah wasn't at a singles' conference, wearing a name tag that said, "Hi! My name is Becky, and I'm available!" You've seen them, the ones with the little tear-off phone numbers. Instead, she was going about her daily chores, getting water from the city well in the evening when all the women came to draw water. At the well a man asked her for a drink of water. She not only gave him a drink but also filled the trough for his camels. The man immediately said, "You! You're the one!" That night before Rebekah went to sleep, she was engaged to a rich man she had never met before!

I've often wondered how many single people at get-togethers go around offering each other cups of coffee, tea, or punch, secretly hoping that one day someone will respond, "You! You're the one!"

Perhaps your fantasy is more of a *Solomon fantasy*.[6] The Lord came to Solomon in a dream one night and told him to ask for whatever he wanted and it would be granted to him. If God were to offer you that same deal, what would you ask for? Money? Fame? A job? A house? A relationship? A new face or body?

Or maybe you have a

Hezekiah fantasy. You wish to be healed from a terminal illness.[7]

Joseph fantasy. You wish for an unexpected promotion to an important job.[8]

Hannah fantasy. You wish to have a child.[9]

Peter fantasy. You wish to "walk on water," doing the impossible.[10]

Paul and Silas fantasy. You wish God would free you from whatever your prison (rut) is.[11]

There's nothing wrong with the occasional fantasy or moment of wishful thinking. And there's nothing wrong with praying about our wants and desires. In fact God instructs us to tell him what we want. But sometimes we don't get what we ask for and we wonder why.

Often what we ask for may not be good for us, and the Lord in his infinite wisdom knows that. In his love for us, he may answer our request with a no. It isn't always easy to thank him for the no, but if we are willing to accept his answer, we often will see how our fantasies would have turned to ashes if exposed to the fires of reality.

PROBLEMS WITH FANTASIES

Whatever your personal fantasy, if it becomes the driving force of your life, your reason for living, an obsession, you're headed for real trouble. Living with fantasies is a rut that can lead to many problems.

Fantasies Give Us Selective Perception

When I was first divorced many years ago, I thought that I would never again remarry. I had been deeply hurt, and I began to think of marriage as a synonym for pain. But as time went by, I found that I began to heal and was ready for a friendship with a man. I found a terrific friend, and we had great times together. If our relationship had problems, we ignored them because we enjoyed the other parts of our relationship so much.

As I rebuilt my life, I discovered that I had a lot to learn about relationships and began making changes in my life. I began to think that maybe I even was ready to consider marriage! Somewhere along the way my friendship had turned into a dating relationship, and that was fine with me by then.

My friend and I had been dating for almost two years when we began talking about the possibility of getting married. Secretly I told God that I was finally ready. Then one day about a week before my birthday, my friend said he was going to take me to dinner at a fancy restaurant and had something important to talk with me about. I had a hunch I knew what it was. I bought a new dress, fixed my hair, and drove to the restaurant where I was to meet him.

We had a lovely dinner. The food was terrific, the conversation witty, and the company special. Finally it was time to talk.

"You're a very special person," he began.

This is it, I thought, trying to remain calm and poised as I gave the appropriate response, "You're terrific, too."

"I love you a lot," he said, sort of matter-of-factly.

"I love you," I responded with a tender smile.

"We've really gone beyond just friendship in our relationship," he continued. "And what we have is so great, that I couldn't ever just be friends again."

"I know," I sighed blissfully, trying to be patient through this long buildup. (I wished he would just hurry up and ask me!)

"So, I guess the next step is marriage," he explained seriously.

"Well, I suppose so," I said, trying not to seem overly eager since he was obviously going to do this at his own pace. I had just opened my mouth to accept his proposal when he finished what he had to say.

"And since I'm not ready to get married, I'm not going to see you anymore!"

I was stunned. Somehow I managed to finish my coffee, make my excuses, and get out of the restaurant without losing my composure. Driving home, I was furious. How dare he walk out of my life after two years? Why had God allowed me to be hurt again? I cried. I prayed. I pouted. I could see myself growing old alone and unwanted. I felt sorry for myself. Then I felt angry again. Finally, emotionally spent, I turned to God quietly, questioningly. And God spoke to me.

"Bobbie," I could almost hear him say audibly, "do you want a second divorce?"

I thought, *This is the second conversation that isn't going well tonight!*

But God continued speaking. "If I gave you what you want, you would only be hurt. You're not ready."

I argued that I was ready. I could name a dozen ways I had grown since my divorce and at least a dozen things I had learned about relationships. But God seemed to keep saying that it was I, not the guy, who wasn't ready. Finally I figured it out. There must be a few more little things I needed to work on. Maybe if I knew what they were, I could fix them and get the guy back in a couple of days. "Show me, Lord," I prayed. God pulled out a list so long I protested, "God, I'll be eighty-two years old before I work through that list!"

But God was right. I wasn't ready. When I finally accepted the fact that the relationship with my friend was truly over, I could honestly evaluate it. I now have no doubt that if I had married this guy, we wouldn't have been able to make the marriage work. There was too much wrong between us. Can you believe that I seriously considered marrying a man who couldn't stand kids? Me, with two young sons? Imagine someone like me, who needs the security of a steady paycheck, married to a man who changed jobs every six months and spends money he doesn't have.

My fantasy had clouded my perception of reality. I saw only what I had wanted to see and ignored some very real problems.

Fantasies Sacrifice the Present

Living for fantasies often leads to sacrificing the here and now. Single people waiting for Mr. or Ms. Wonderful tend to put off a lot of things. They don't get involved in community events or church activities because they don't want to have too many evenings tied up, just in case they start a relationship. Or they won't go out with same-sex friends because they need to wait at home for that magic phone call. They end up spending Saturday evenings alone at home just because they didn't have a date.

Several years ago I knew a woman who dreamed of running a marathon. She worked at her dream, training, eating the correct foods, running every day, and watching her weight. Finally she signed up to run in a nearby marathon and began to train even more intensely.

As the day of the contest approached, she announced that she was going to quit running after the marathon. She explained, "I've discovered that running has taken over my life. I can't enjoy some of my favorite things, like tennis, swimming, volleyball, or football, because I'm afraid I'll twist my ankle. I can't eat what I want or stay up late to watch a program on television because I need to stay fit and get enough rest. I can't do what I want to do today because I'm waiting to run the marathon in three weeks."

A lot of people live their lives the same way. They don't enjoy what they have because it isn't what they want! They can't enjoy a friendship because it isn't a romance. They can't enjoy a dating relationship because it isn't a marriage. They can't enjoy an evening out with friends if they don't have a special person in their lives.

Fantasies can cause us to throw away the good things we have right now. And that kind of living is harmful. We need to live in the present, enjoying the good things God has given us for today.[12]

Fantasies Foster Unrealistic Expectations

People who spend a lot of time wishing for their fantasies to come true begin to build a set of unrealistic expectations against which they measure reality. Reality often falls far short of the fantasy. Even if part of the fantasy comes true, the dreamer is disappointed because it isn't all it should be. Unrealistic expectations can be a terrible trap.

Carla has a fantasy that one day Mr. Wonderful will come into her life. She has visualized it so many times that she knows exactly how it will happen. A friend will introduce them, and they will go to CoCo's Restaurant for coffee and begin sharing instantly at a feeling level. About an hour into the conversation, the man will reach over, take her hand, look deeply into her eyes, and say huskily, "Do you know how long I have waited for a woman like you?" And that will be the beginning of the world's greatest love relationship.

Carla wants that fantasy so much that every time she meets a new man, she invites him to CoCo's Restaurant and waits for the fantasy to begin. When it doesn't happen the way she hoped, she goes home sick with disappointment and never sees the man again, no matter how nice he had seemed.

Karen has a fantasy that a very rich man will fall in love with her and resolve her financial problems. Even though she admits that this daydream won't necessarily come true, she resists dating men who don't earn large salaries. She would rather spend an evening alone, planning dream vacations she will take with her rich husband when he shows up. She has mentally designed the custom home she wants to live in. She has a list of important people she wants to be their friends. She often spends a Saturday window-shopping at I. Magnin so she will know what she wants to buy, when she can afford it.

Karen might get her fantasy, who knows? But in the meantime, her fantasy is costing her several years of her life.

Fantasies Inhibit Growth

As long as we live in our fantasies, we don't need to grow or change. Alice says that when she finds a relationship, she will start being a neat housekeeper. Meanwhile, her house always looks as if a tornado hit it. I wonder if she'll ever have a relationship if a man sees her house first.

Ned says that if he ever finds the right woman, he'll learn to watch his language and temper. Meanwhile, he offends most people, and no woman has stayed around long enough to get to know him well.

The fantasy world has no unsolvable problems, no immovable obstacles. Love conquers all. When we live for the fantasy, we see little need for self-development. When we live for the fantasy, we ignore the need to take an honest look at ourselves and recognize the areas that need to change, that need to be shaped by God's loving hand.

HOPES, EXPECTATIONS, AND GOALS

When we live in the rut of fantasy life, we subconsciously admit that we are dissatisfied and want our lives to change. But how do we get out of the rut? How do we make things happen in our lives?

Jerry wants a birthday party. He *hopes* his friends surprise him with a party on his next birthday.

Tom wants to be a leader. He *expects* an appointment to the governing board of his church.

Cathy wants to play golf. She sets a *goal* to play golf every Saturday morning for the next two months.

These three people want something to happen in their lives, but each approaches that "something" from a different perspective: Jerry hopes, Tom expects, and Cathy sets a goal. Let's look at the differences in these approaches.

Hopes

To *hope* is to want something that is out of our control. When we hope, we don't take the responsibility for making something happen. When we hope, we basically give over to someone else the power of determining the level of satisfaction we experience. If our hopes are realized, we're happy; if they aren't, we're disappointed. Solomon said it best in one of his proverbs: "Hope deferred makes the heart sick, but desire fulfilled is a tree of life."[13]

Have you ever realized that sometimes when we resort

just to hoping something will happen, we are relying on someone else to read our minds or remember an obscure hint we may have dropped in previous conversations? Jerry's hope for a surprise birthday party hinged on his friends remembering a comment he made at a surprise party he had given for one of them. He had offhandedly joked that he himself had never been surprised with a party on his birthday. He hoped that one of them had noted his hint and had begun right then to plan a party for him.

We don't always share our hopes with others. Our hopes may not be the choice of the other people involved! With hope, there are no guarantees, no plans to make things happen; there is only waiting and usually being disappointed, because people will frequently let us down, and not always gently!

Jerry is sad a lot of the time because his hopes are not often realized. He feels disappointed and at times unloved because no one cares enough to fulfill his hopes.

Expectations

An *expectation* is looking for something that we feel is due us, something we feel others owe us. Tom expects things to happen to him. He feels that his church owes him an appointment, that his sister owes him respect, that his boss owes him recognition, and that his family owes him expensive gifts on holidays. Because he actively expects these things, Tom is rarely surprised or excited when nice things happen in his life. He merely accepts them as his rightful due. On the other hand, Tom is often disappointed and angry when his expectations aren't fulfilled because other people don't always agree with Tom about what they "owe" him!

Maybe Tom needs to follow the advice of the apostle Paul, who says, "Owe nothing to anyone, except to love one another."[14] As long as Tom goes around acting like a bill collector, he will continue to alienate people, even his friends.

If our family, friends, and dating partners know and agree with our expectations, then we may not have serious problems. But often our expectations are not well thought out and are unrealistic. Unrealistic expectations lead to critical attitudes and are unfair to the other people in the relationship.

Goals

Cathy wants to play golf. She could have waited around *hoping* for someone to ask her to play. She could have *expected* her friend Joyce to be her partner every Saturday morning and been angry whenever Joyce had other plans. But Cathy didn't want to play these games; she wanted to play golf! So she set a *goal:* to play golf every Saturday morning for two months. She then shared her goal with friends until she found several people who played golf or wanted to learn. She then systematically filled in her calendar until she had a partner every Saturday for two months. Cathy even found a few people who could fill in on short notice if one of Cathy's "dates" had to cancel. She had met her goal.

Converting Hopes and Expectations to Goals

Hopes and expectations are passive; they place the responsibility on other people to make things happen. Setting goals is active; when we set a goal we take responsibility for meeting our own needs and making things happen.

If we look carefully at our hopes and expectations, we recognize that some of them are merely desires to be loved and accepted. When we don't feel secure, we may spend a lot of time hoping or demanding that people do loving things for us. Jerry's hopes and Tom's expectations reveal their need for love and acceptance.

Once we eliminate those hopes and expectations that are really desires to be loved and accepted, we can begin to convert the remaining hopes and expectations into goals. Do you want a new home, a different job, a skill, a degree, or more friends? Do something about it! Start a savings account. Send out resumés. Learn to ski. Take a class. Plan a vacation. Invite a friend over for dinner.

Recognize that some goals can be accomplished quickly; others may take years. But as a friend of mine puts it: "The difference between what you *are* and what you *become* is what you *do!*"

You can get out of your rut. Take action. Start today.

LEARN TO RISK

✔ SELF-ASSESSMENT AND FOLLOW-UP

1. Rate your fantasy life. Write the appropriate number in front of each sentence: 3 means you always do this; 2 means you sometimes do this; and 1 means you almost never do this.

   ___ a. I spend a lot of time daydreaming.
   ___ b. I'm basically waiting for a partner to fulfill my fantasies.
   ___ c. I'm not really happy with what I have because it isn't what I truly want.
   ___ d. I'm often disappointed with my friends.
   ___ e. I sit home waiting to be called and invited out.
   ___ f. I don't set goals; I just hope things will work out.
   ___ g. My fantasies are better than my realities.
   ___ h. I don't feel satisfied with my life.
   ___ i. I wish someone would rescue me.
   ___ j. I wish I had more friends.
   ___ **Total points**

Add up your score.

   10–15 Your feet are planted firmly on the ground. You probably are fairly realistic, and you probably take charge of your life.
   16–25 You sometimes take charge and sometimes dream. You'll be okay, but more of life is just waiting for you.
   26–30 You may want to rethink your choices because you are probably just wasting your life waiting for something good to happen!

2. Start a journal that will reflect your thoughts about the main ideas in each chapter of this book. Write about issues with which you agree or disagree. Explore how the ideas in each chapter may be true in your own life.

3. Make a dream list by quickly finishing the following statement as many times as you can. "I wish that...."

RELEASE THE FANTASIES

4. Place an X in front of those statements that are really desires to be loved and accepted.

5. Convert four or five of the remaining dreams into real goals. Write the goals in your journal, making sure each goal is broken into measurable steps (how much, how many, how long, etc.). Then assign completion dates to each step. Start working on these today. Check on your progress in two weeks.

6. Reflect on the most significant relationship in your life. Is your predominate style in that relationship one of hoping, expecting, or setting goals and working together to reach them? What changes can you make in that relationship to improve the interaction?

GROUP INTERACTION

1. **Discussion.** Use the following discussion starters to get everyone involved in the discussion. Work in groups of 5–10, giving each person a chance to complete the first statement before the group moves on to the next one. If a person is uncomfortable sharing, that person may pass.

   a. My favorite fantasy is. . . .
   b. I wish I could have the same experience as (name a Bible character) had when (describe the story briefly).
   c. I wish I could. . . .
   d. I used to want to. . . .
   e. What I expect of a friend is. . . .
   f. What I expect of a dating partner is. . . .
   g. I feel most loved and accepted when. . . .
   h. I show that I love and accept someone when. . . .
   i. I have unreasonable expectations when. . . .
   j. One of my goals is to. . . .

2. **Dream List.** Make a dream list (or use the one you compiled for your self-assessment) by quickly writing as many endings as you can for the following sentence: "I wish that. . . ." Then share your list with a partner and see how your dreams compare. Discuss which dreams are

really desires for love and acceptance. Then brainstorm about ways to meet those desires in a productive and healthy way.

3. **Character Exploration.** Work in groups of four or five. Think of other types of fantasies that are based on the experiences of Bible characters. What lessons can we learn from their lives? Share in the large group when it is reconvened.

4. **Charades.** Form two groups. Together with the group members, write a list of common fantasies. Taking turns, act out one of the fantasies, getting the other group to guess the fantasy.

2
Live Beyond Rejection

Rejection is
—telling a joke and having no one laugh.
—going for an interview and not getting the job.
—giving a "warm fuzzy" and receiving a "cold prickly."
—saying "I love you" and having the other person say, "that's nice."
—having someone special walk out of our lives.

Most of us have experienced rejection of one kind or another. Some of us have been devastated as a result of the experience. Others of us have survived with little more than a period of sadness.

Visualize a pair of medal-winning ice skaters, whose moves on the ice demonstrate the long hours they have spent learning to trust one another and perfecting their knowledge of one another's moves. As a team they are perfectly balanced, but at times one or the other may be individually off balance as he or she counterbalances or supports the other.

Can you imagine what would happen if during a particularly difficult routine one partner were simply to let go and walk away? The remaining partner probably would flail around, stumble, fall, and possibly get hurt.

That's similar to what happens when someone we are counting on for support decides to withdraw and walk away. The rejected person is left to stumble and fall while trying to regain his or her balance. The resulting injuries are emotional, but the pain may also be physical. The pain of rejection is usually something we remember vividly and work hard to avoid.

UNHEALTHY DEFENSE STRATEGIES

People who have been rejected recently or who have never gotten over the trauma of a rejection experience can be extremely sensitive. They may feel seriously rejected if someone doesn't like them, if someone criticizes them, or if they feel they have failed to live up to others' expectations. These people become so afraid of being rejected that they build elaborate defense strategies to avoid the possibility of ever being rejected again. They get stuck in a rut.

Let's look at some of these defense strategies.

Perceive Rejection That Isn't There

Several years ago I met a terrific guy who worked in an office near mine. We began talking on our breaks or lunch hours, and I began to depend on seeing him during the day because he seemed genuinely interested in me as a person. After a couple of weeks, I found I wanted to discuss a problem with him during lunch hour, but I didn't want to seem pushy and demanding of his time. I thought about how I might approach him. Finally I decided I could prepare a picnic lunch and suggest that we go outside and sit in the park to talk privately. Having selected an approach, I waited for him to drop by my desk.

Sure enough he came by on his break. I took a deep breath and started: "Steve, I just had a great idea. How about having a picnic in the park tomorrow at lunchtime? I'll bring the lunch, and we can talk."

Before I could finish my sentence, I saw a funny look on his face. I thought to myself, *I've just blown it. He thinks I'm pushy, and he doesn't know how to tell me he doesn't want to have lunch with me. He'll never talk with me again.* I felt awful! Trying to undo the damage, I quickly started over. "Listen, just forget it. It was just an idea I had, nothing important. Besides, I couldn't have lunch tomorrow anyway. I need to do some shopping."

Steve patiently pulled up a chair beside my desk and

responded. "Let me get this straight. First you invite me to lunch, then before I can say anything, you uninvite me. Right?"

Hurriedly I explained that I had wanted to talk with him but didn't know how to ask him if he had time, so I had thought of the picnic idea. But when I saw a look of rejection on his face, I knew that I had been presumptuous. I withdrew the offer in order to save him the embarrassment of having to tell me no.

Steve just shook his head. "Don't try to be a mind reader," he cautioned me. "The reason I hesitated a little was that I've been trying to lose weight before I go on vacation. Do you know what people usually bring to picnics? Potato chips, potato salad, fried chicken, sandwiches, cookies—all the things I can't have. I was trying to decide whether to say I would bring my own lunch, break my diet, or hope that you would bring something I could eat. It took a few minutes to process those alternatives. I was never considering saying I wouldn't have lunch with you. The only question was what I would eat!"

It was a lesson I never forgot.

We often are so afraid of being rejected that we anticipate rejection. We end up reading rejection into the most innocent interactions.

A friend of mine puts it this way: "We often frisk the dialogue for the fingerprints of connotation." Solomon says it another way: "What a shame—yes, how stupid!—to decide before knowing the facts!"[1]

This first strategy is unhealthy because if we are that easily offended, people will begin to stay away from us so they don't have to watch their words all of the time to keep from hurting us.

Reject Others Before They Can Reject Us

This second defense strategy can take one of two forms: Reject them because we know we won't like them, or reject them because we know they won't like us.

Annie walked into a PTA meeting for the first time and looked around the room. She could tell just by looking that these weren't her kind of people. They all seemed too poised, too confident, too happy, too friendly. She knew if she stayed, she would feel out of place and uncomfortable because she didn't feel poised, confident, or friendly. She turned around and went home.

Peter walked into the same meeting and also left. He saw the group as a bunch of casually dressed, average-looking losers.

Neither Annie nor Peter stayed long enough to talk with anyone or to validate their perceptions. They simply rejected the group. Both were too afraid of being rejected in new situations to stay and risk reaching out.

This defense strategy also leads to problems. If this is typical behavior for Annie and Peter, they probably don't have very many friends and they probably won't take many risks in relationships.

Reject Ourselves

Have you ever had dinner in a home that looked as if it were featured in *House Beautiful* magazine? The table setting was elegant, the centerpiece fabulous, and the meal terrific. Then before you could fully enjoy the meal, the hostess started. "I'm sorry about the meal. The gravy is a bit salty, the meat is too well done, and I had to use frozen peas instead of fresh because the market didn't have any fresh." From the soup to dessert, she pointed out something wrong with every dish. You almost became convinced that the terrific meal *was* terrible.

People who use this defense strategy are so afraid of rejection that they reject themselves before someone else can. "I'm sorry" is their favorite phrase.

The problem with this strategy is that the needy person often ends up with a double rejection: Not only has the person rejected himself or herself, but other people may become so irritated by the constant apologizing and self-criticism that they may purposely avoid the needy person.

If God has accepted us as valuable and lovable human beings, then what right do we have to put ourselves down and pretend to be unacceptable?[2] We need to have a positive self-concept, to assess who we are and what we are becoming. If we don't like some things about ourselves, we have the ability to change our attitudes, behaviors, and ideas. We can choose to change and grow!

Become Immobilized

Paula is so terrified of being rejected that she goes to great lengths to avoid disagreeing with anyone. She usually waits until people have said what they think before she will chime in and agree. She often gets caught contradicting herself when she is with people who don't agree with each other. Paula will never express a preference about what activity to do, where to go to eat, what to watch on television, or how to spend an evening. Most of her friends find that she's more of a passenger than a partner in the relationship, and they eventually drift away from her to find someone who can contribute to a relationship.

Paula is immobilized in relationships. Her defense strategy doesn't work. She thinks she has several good friendships, but in reality they are little more than casual relationships. She needs to learn that in loving friendships, people are free to be themselves, even if that means disagreeing. The New Testament reminds us that friendships should last through disagreements. After the apostle Paul spoke boldly to the church in Galatia, he asked them, "Have I now become your enemy by telling you the truth?"[3]

Become Egocentric

Aaron is so afraid of being rejected that he doesn't let people get near him. He focuses so completely on himself that he doesn't let anyone else suspect that he needs or desires any interaction from them. He dominates any conversation with his opinions, experiences, ideas, and suggestions. He never asks for recommendations or allows any input into the plans for an outing. He quickly pooh-poohs any disagreements and refuses even to consider that he might be wrong. He misinterprets acquiescence with his plans as approval and winning an argument with being right.

Aaron is basically imprisoned by his own defense strategy. His self-centeredness and self-stroking has alienated his acquaintances, who get the message that they aren't needed, wanted, or valued. The New Testament teaches that love doesn't have an inflated view of itself, doesn't look after its own interests.[4] Love doesn't go around patting itself on the back. Love reaches out and gives to others. Therefore people who become egocentric end up being lonely and rejected.

Hold Negative Feelings Inside

Some people are so afraid of rejection that they will appear to tolerate major differences or even offensive behavior. Joel picks his nose, tells rotten jokes, yells at other drivers, and embarrasses Gina in public. But she overlooks all of these annoyances because she is so hungry for a relationship.

Ken keeps his negative feelings inside. He is organized and a very neat housekeeper. He feels that if everything has its place and is in it, his life is in good shape. When he started dating Cindy, he was secretly appalled at the state of her house. The first time he saw it, he figured she just had gotten behind in her housework. But each time he came over to her house, it was the same. He would find newspapers and soda cans strewn across the living-room floor, dirty dishes and glasses stashed under the couch, and children's dirty clothes draped over most of the furniture. It always appeared that Cindy had at least three projects underway, ranging from a jigsaw puzzle to dressmaking. But because Ken found Cindy to be a terrific woman in every other way, he excused her one "fault."

Ken realized that he was uncomfortable in such a messy house, but rather than talk to Cindy about it, he started having her come over to his house for their dates. At first Cindy felt intimidated by the spotless atmosphere at Ken's place, but eventually she began to feel more at home and behaved accordingly. She often left her iced-tea glass on the end table in the living room or tossed the dish towel on the kitchen table after helping with the dishes. As soon as Cindy left for home, Ken would jump up and clean up after her, usually feeling somewhat irritated that she didn't respect his desires for a neat house. But even while he felt irritated, he would remind himself that she was a genuinely good person with whom he enjoyed spending time.

Cindy and Ken dated for months, and all the time Ken pretended that he liked Cindy just as she was. Then one

Saturday he had to work overtime. Cindy suggested that if he would give her his key, she would go over to his house and prepare dinner for them both so they could still have the evening together. Ken agreed. Perhaps things would have been all right, except for the fact that Ken had forgotten some papers that his boss needed, so his boss followed Ken home to pick them up.

When Ken opened the door to his house, he couldn't believe his eyes. The living room, which he had left in perfect order, was a disaster. The Saturday newspaper was strewn all over the floor; dirty dishes covered the kitchen counters; and a load of washing (not his) was dumped on the couch.

As soon as his boss left, Ken blew up. In the first place, how dare she do this to him? In the second place, how in the world could one person do this much damage in one short afternoon? And in the third place, did she go out of her way to be messy or did it just come naturally?

Cindy never understood just what she had done! She knew that Ken was neat, yet she hadn't known that her messiness bothered him because he had never said anything. So what was the real problem? When Ken said that their relationship was over, Cindy felt betrayed and confused.

This defense strategy is also unhealthy. By holding negative feelings inside, the person gives silent permission for the continuation of those behaviors. The end result of this defense strategy is rejection by the other person.

Gina and Ken need to learn to risk being honest about their negative feelings, to risk speaking the truth in love.[5] If we want our relationships to grow and be healthy, we need to talk to each other about our differences rather than passively accept them.

Hold People Off at Arm's Length

People who are afraid of rejection are often obnoxious, abrasive, unfriendly, or critical. Sara refuses to date anyone more than once so that she won't get emotionally involved and be vulnerable to being hurt again. She is unfriendly not only because she doesn't reach out but also because she resists anyone else's attempts to befriend her.

If Andy feels as if he is getting close to a woman, he

usually sabotages the relationship and behaves in strange ways that are guaranteed to make her terminate their dating relationship.

Both Sara and Andy need to learn that holding people off is not a healthy way to cope with their fears of being rejected. They need to choose a better way, to risk allowing people to get close to them.

Obviously none of these seven defense strategies works! In fact, they all end up causing the very thing they are trying to avoid—rejection. When we use any of these defense strategies, we tell the world that we are operating out of fear rather than confidence. We need to learn to let go of our fear and experience the freedom to be the persons God has created us to be.[6]

HEALTHY WAYS TO COPE WITH REJECTION

All of us at one time or another find that we are deeply disappointed and hurt by the actions of others. But we can choose how we respond. We can use unhealthy defense strategies, or we can take the following steps to cope with hurt and rejection in healthy ways.

Recognize That Rejection Is Inevitable

Unfortunately not everyone is going to like us, approve of our choices, or respond to our overtures of friendship. But that's okay. We don't like everyone else either!

Melvin wore his best suit and took a perfectly typed resumé to the job interview, but he still didn't get the job. Melvin was disappointed, but he knew he had tried his best.

Grace saw her former boyfriend going into "their" pizza place one night and felt again some of the rejection she had felt when they stopped dating. But she quickly reminded herself that she had to expect to see him again and probably with someone else, since they both lived in such a small town.

Most of us can identify with Melvin and Grace's feelings of rejection because we all have felt rejected at one time or another. But we need to remind ourselves that it's up to us to determine how seriously hurt we are going to be by these rejections, many of which need not be devastating. People won't always take our advice, like our tastes in art or music, enjoy our favorite foods, or want to be with us. We are all individuals with unique needs, wants, and tastes, which sometimes are not the same as others'. That's okay! In fact, that's nice because then we have so much to share with other people.

Acknowledge That Rejection Hurts and Deal with the Pain

Eileen had a new male friend. They laughed a lot together, enjoyed doing the same things, spent several evenings a week together, sharing ideas, feelings, projects, and activities. He got along well with her kids and her friends, and she with his. Along the way Eileen fell in love. One night when her friend kissed her good night, she reached her arms up, hugged him close, and whispered, "I love you."

"Let's not rush things," he responded, gently but unmistakably pushing her away.

Eileen felt as if she had been physically struck.

Rejection hurts, a lot! Rejection sometimes feels as if we are getting spit at in the face, hit on the head, punched in the stomach, and cut off at the knees all at the same time. Rejection triggers embarrassment, self-reproach, self-doubt, humiliation, fear, loneliness, and physical pain. So when you are having a rejection experience, acknowledge the pain and take care of yourself.

In her book *Brief Encounters*, Emily Coleman suggests several ways to defuse the initial pain of rejection.[7]

1. Tune into your body. Conduct a thorough mental inventory to see how your body is experiencing the rejection. What changes can you identify? Start with your feet. Are they suddenly warmer or colder? How about your legs and knees? Are they wobbly? Check your thighs and stomach. Any cramps or nausea? What about your chest and back? Any pain or tenseness? Check your arms and hands. Are they clammy? What about your face? Flushed? Is your head or neck tense?

2. Define the pain. Once you have identified the pain, try to isolate and define it. If your chest hurts, in what way does it hurt? Is the pain sharp or dull? Hot or cold? Does it go across your chest or stay on one side? Does it go from the front of your chest all the way to your back? If you could see it, what shape would it have? How big? How heavy would it be?

"For me the pain seems to be a cold, hard lump, varying in size from three to four inches in diameter to as big as eight or nine inches in diameter," David shares. "It's located right in the center of the left side of my chest. It feels as if it goes all the way to my back and reaches the front of my rib cage. Sometimes it feels as if there are little arms of pain that reach out from the main mass, one to my stomach, one to my head, one to my back."

David has learned to define the pain. He has found that by concentrating on the physical feeling of the pain, the size of the pain seems to begin to shrink. He imagines the pain becoming smaller and smaller, and soon he feels a lessening of the tension and pressure in his body.

Once you have defined the pain or tension in your body, you can take steps to alleviate it. Deliberately take slow, deep breaths to ease pain in your chest and back. Take a warm shower or soak in a hot tub to relax your muscles. Sit or lie down, practicing systematic relaxation to relieve tension and weakness in your knees and legs. Sip a cup of bouillon or eat a cracker to lessen the nausea.

Of course the real relief will come when you have passed through the worst of the emotional pain of the rejection experience. But listening to your body and taking some simple physical actions to diminish the pain will help.

3. Check your breathing. Is it shallow or deep? Hurried or slow? Take several slow, deep breaths. I often find that when I'm stressed, shocked, or hurt, my chest begins to hurt. When I check it out, I find that I'm actually holding my breath. I have to think consciously about expelling the air.

4. Check your heartbeat. Is it rapid or slow? Pounding loudly or barely beating? If it's rapid or pounding, focus on relaxing enough to slow the heartbeat back down to normal. If it's barely beating, take several deep breaths and try to unlock some of the fear.

5. Stop the mental tape recorder. As soon as you experience rejection, your mind turns on little recorders that begin to play back the worst possible tapes. "How could you have been so stupid as to believe in that person?" the recording asks. "You dummy, what makes you think you'll ever have a relationship? You sure do know how to pick 'em, don't you? You should have kept your feelings to yourself! You knew better than to trust people. Now you'll be alone for the rest of your life. No one is ever going to love you again!" On and on goes the recorder, not just once, but over and over until you begin to believe the messages and sink into depression.

When you are aware that your mental tape recording is giving you negative messages, stop the process and say to yourself, "I will not think destructive thoughts. I reject them." Talk back to the recorder, countering the negative messages with positive ones. Then concentrate on pleasant things, things that inspire you, uplift you, and encourage you.[8]

6. Find affirmation. When you've suffered an emotional injury, you need to be taken care of. Accepting comfort may not be easy for some people, especially if they usually give to others rather than receive from them. But you need to allow yourself to be comforted.

When you have been rejected, you may suffer from a desperate need for several types of affirmation. These might include compliments, recognition, attention, appreciation, affection, and touch. But how do you find these affirmations?

Go to a friend and admit your need for a hug, either a physical one or an emotional one. Spend time with people who appreciate you and whom you like. Select several close friends who can be instant affirmers and keep their phone numbers near your telephone and on a card in your wallet for quick reference when you need to contact someone who cares.

Attend small-group sessions sponsored by a church, a singles' ministry, self-help organizations, or a counseling center. Talk with your family and friends about the positive things you accomplish every day, even if you don't feel those accomplishments are very important right now.

Take extra care with your appearance. Wear clothes that make you feel attractive. Have your hair cut or styled in a new way.

Do things that feel good on a sensory level. Eat your favorite foods (in small amounts). Wear a nice cologne. Take a walk in a forested area. Spray the house with fresh scents or open a jar of potpourri. Take a warm bubble bath. Listen to classical music, hang wind chimes on the patio, or go to a concert. Buy a picture for your bedroom wall, or paint the living room a new color. Take in the sights, sounds, tastes, and smells around you.

Of course, doing these things for yourself and by yourself is not as satisfying as being loved by the one you love. These are poor substitutes. But they *are* substitutes. A hungry person may crave steak and lobster, but vegetable soup is better than starvation. And substituted affirmation is better than starving yourself to the point of being ready to die from a lack of love.

Decide What Was Rejected

In spite of how it feels, rejection is most often much less personal than it seems. Most often it's not *you* who is being rejected; it's what you offer the other person. Eileen's friend was not rejecting her as a friend or person; he just wasn't ready for a more intimate or romantic relationship.

Valerie and Kyle hit it off well right away. They always stood around and talked after church on Sunday evenings for several minutes. They laughed, enjoyed each other's company, and generally had a great time. Then one Sunday evening Valerie asked Kyle to go over to the coffee shop for a cup of coffee. He looked at his watch, said he had to go, and dashed off. Valerie thought he just had plans, so she waited until the next week and repeated her invitation. The same scenario occurred. This time Valerie felt a little put off. But when he dashed off again the third week, she felt rejected! She waited a couple of weeks, during which they continued to sit together in church and talk afterward. Finally Valerie confronted Kyle.

"Just what's going on?" she asked. "We seem to have such a good time, but the minute I suggest that we go across the street for coffee, you dash off. What gives? I feel rejected!"

"Rejected!" Kyle laughed. "I work Sunday nights. I can't stay. In fact, I've been late to work for the last two months because I keep talking with you! I'd love to get together. How about lunch next Sunday?"

Sometimes rejection is a response to a specific time frame. Someone may not want or be ready to accept your gesture of friendship at a specific time but may seek you out at a later time, ready to accept what had once been rejected. Ted was newly divorced and emotionally scarred. He was a long way from being ready for a new relationship when he met Sally. Sally, on the other hand, was ready for a new relationship and found Ted to be the kind of sensitive, caring person she appreciated. She reached out to him, but he kept his distance, even though he obviously enjoyed being with her. Finally Sally recognized that Ted needed a lot more time to heal. She gave up any expectations for a romantic relationship and just continued to be a good friend to Ted.

Four years later Ted found that he had come to a healthy place in his life and was ready for a romantic relationship. He turned to his best friend, Sally, for that relationship. It doesn't always happen that way. Frequently if we aren't ready for a particular level of interaction, the other person moves on and finds someone who is. But that doesn't make it right to force a relationship that isn't working for both parties. Being honest enough to admit that we aren't ready for a deeper level of interaction is more kind than going too fast into a relationship that isn't all it could be.

Sometimes it's merely the level of interaction that the other person rejects; sometimes our timing is just off. But how are you going to find out what is being rejected? Ask! This is risky but necessary because we aren't mind readers. Learn to ask gentle questions that help you learn what the other person is responding to. An honest answer is always easier to cope with than our uncertain speculations.

Find Out Why You've Been Rejected

If you have been rejected often and find it hard to recover, look for the reasons. Sometimes your behavior or attitudes may cause you to be rejected. When I finally became willing to risk in relationships after surviving a divorce, I started dating. Over the next four years I had three serious relationships, each of which ended the same way. One night I reflected over those relationships and discovered something interesting. I had been selecting the wrong type of man to date. I was attracted to independent men, but I had gone overboard and had picked three men who were so independent that they didn't need or want serious relationships. In fact, all three of those men are still unattached fifteen years later. I was doing something that was causing me to end up rejected.

Perhaps some behaviors or habits in your life turn people off. Maybe you are using unhealthy defense strategies and are creating rejection around you. Maybe you are less than skillful in communication or relational skills.

A friend of mine told me he was having trouble with his relationships. Having watched him go through six relationships in a year, I agreed that he had a problem. "I have the first six weeks down pat," he shared. "I know what to say, when to call, what activities to suggest. I have played these six weeks over so many times, I'm good at them." And indeed he was. He could make a woman feel special, cherished, wanted, and loved in six short weeks. He would take her on unusual outings, bring special little gifts like a pine cone with the message, "I missed you when I was walking in the woods." He was an expert at talking on the telephone and making a woman feel understood and valued. He was attentive, fun, and intellectually stimulating for six weeks. But when the woman became more serious, which usually had happened by the end of the six weeks, his polished relational skills fell apart. He didn't know how to handle the interaction, the woman, or himself. He would begin to sabotage the relationship until the woman would end up rejecting him. A couple of weeks later he would start a new relationship. It took my friend a few years to work on his skills so that he could have a relationship that lasted longer than six weeks.

If you suspect something is wrong in your life, pray about it. Ask God to show you what needs to be changed. Ask him to shape you into a godly person, a person who is loving, joyous, patient, good, gentle, kind, and self-controlled.[9]

Check Your Expectations

Probably the biggest problem in relationships is having unrealistic expectations. Do you feel rejected when someone is not ready for the same level of commitment you want? Do you let down your emotional barriers so quickly that others can't keep up? Do you expect others to be skilled in confronting, choosing, and changing, just because you want them to be? Do you expect people to fulfill your desires all of the time? Do you think that a real friend would know what you want and do it for you? Do you fail to communicate your needs and wants, yet hold others accountable for them?

Unrealistic expectations can set us up to feel rejected. Donna approaches every singles' party with the hope that she will look across the crowded room, meet the eyes of Mr. Right, fall instantly in love as the music swells and the crowd mysteriously fades away. She acts accordingly. Donna enters a room, stops just inside the door, and starts scanning the group, expectantly waiting for the magic to happen. Anyone who approaches her is given the quick once over and dismissed if she feels no magic. After every party, Donna cries herself to sleep, feeling unlovable and unwanted, just because Mr. Right never showed up.

Pete is a natural leader, but he feels that instead of having to volunteer his skills, people will naturally recognize them and automatically make him a leader. So he spends a lot of time waiting to be recognized and often feels rejected when others, whom he feels are less competent, volunteered or were chosen as leaders. Pete sets himself up to be rejected.

While we don't often go to such extremes to be rejected, we do sometimes behave like Donna and Pete. We have unrealistic expectations, and we sit back and wait for our dreams and expectations to be fulfilled. People who feel rejected most of the time might need to take a look at their expectations. They might be surprised to discover that they have set expectations so high that no one can ever live up to them, and the end result is feelings of being rejected.

Consider your expectations of your friends. Do you think that just because they are your friends, they must live up to your expectations of what a friend should be like? Cheryl does. According to Cheryl, friends are people who spend lots of quality time with one another, always remember birthdays and little anniversaries, always ensure that holidays aren't spent alone, frequently send little notes and cards as well as bring gifts and flowers to the house, and call one another daily. Cheryl does all of these things for her close friends. But some of her close friends don't share Cheryl's definition of friendship, and they don't think a daily call is essential to a good relationship. Cheryl often feels that her friends are rejecting her because they don't reciprocate her gestures of friendship. Cheryl needs to learn that when her expectations are unrealistic, she will tend to feel rejected more frequently.

When you reach out to others, consider first just what it is you are expecting from them. Are you expecting them to acknowledge your contact? Are you hoping they will take the initiative and aggressively pursue the relationship? Are you praying that they will fall in love with you or become best friends with you? If you realize just what it is you are expecting from the interaction, you can assess whether or not that expectation is realistic. If your expectations are reasonable and realistic, you'll be less likely to be disappointed and feel rejected.

Practice Making Contact Without Having Serious Expectations

You might be surprised at what happens. If someone invites you to a party or to go out for a cup of coffee, go ahead and accept the gesture of friendship, even if you don't plan to marry that person! Don't ask yourself if you feel like going or if it's going to be worth getting dressed up for it. Just go.

Instead of looking for romance, look for joy and happiness. Throw a party. Reach out to help someone else. Phone several friends and talk with each for five minutes. Spend time with friends just for the sheer enjoyment of being with them.

Recognize That Sometimes the Problem Is the Other Person's

I didn't learn this until I was almost thirty. On the second night of a personal-growth seminar, we all participated in a nonverbal exercise. We lined up in two lines, facing each other. As we stood in front of each person, we had to vote on the type of contact we would like to have with him or her. If we held up one finger, we wanted no contact. Two fingers meant a handshake. Three fingers meant a hug. We then followed the vote with the appropriate action and stepped to the left, facing a new partner. All of a sudden I realized that the next person I would be facing was a big, tall guy named Craig. Already within a day and a half, he had managed to alienate virtually everyone in the group. He had been sarcastic, rude, mocking, sullen, and belligerent. I stepped to the left and faced Craig.

Acting on what I thought to be a generous impulse, I held up three fingers. Craig held up one! Embarrassed, we shook hands and quickly stepped to the left and faced new partners. But inwardly I was furious. How dare he reject the only person in the whole room who was willing to reach out to him. I hoped that no one else would reach out to him! It would serve him right if everyone else voted "no contact" with him. I determined that I would avoid him for the rest of the week.

After that first rush of anger, I realized that I was hurt. I had been rejected, rejected by the "worst" person at the seminar. If Craig didn't want any contact with me, then probably no one else did either. In fact, I told myself self-pityingly, those people who had voted to hug me were probably just trying to be as generous as I had tried to be toward Craig. I felt like the laughingstock of the whole seminar. I was crushed.

During the remaining days of the week-long seminar, we shared our struggles, laughed, cried, hugged, applauded, encouraged, and confronted. By the end of the week we had formed strong bonds. When the seminar was over, we stood around crying and hugging one another, clearly reluctant to go home. I felt a tap on my shoulder, and turning around, I found Craig. "Could I have that hug now?" he asked, grinning tentatively.

As we hugged, I confessed: "I was really hurt when you rejected me." Craig looked surprised. "What do you mean? I didn't reject you. I knew what kind of a fool I had been making of myself. I knew that no one in the room would want to hug me. I voted no contact all night. I wasn't rejecting you. I was keeping you all from rejecting me!" What a changed perspective!

Sometimes people refuse to accept our offers of friendship, interaction, or even love because they can't handle the possibility of rejection. I have begun to learn to look past the problem behaviors I see in others and understand that underneath we are all alike. What we want most in life is to be loved and accepted. If I can be a loving and accepting person, I can communicate that it's safe to risk with me. When others begin believing me, they usually reach out in friendship. In other words, sometimes people are critical because they want to keep from being criticized. They are standoffish because they don't think others will really like them. They are selfish because they don't think anyone else will consider their feelings or desires. Basically they just want to be loved but are afraid of being rejected instead.

As we practice healthy ways of coping with rejection, we can learn to get past the rejection experience and on with the business of living a full and abundant life. The most important step in doing that is to ensure that your relationship to God is open, personal, and close. Remember that

- God has a wonderful plan for your life.[10]
- God can work good from any experiences you have.[11]
- You are not a finished product; you are only in the process of becoming.[12]
- God will not reject you.[13]

You can live beyond rejection!

✓ SELF-ASSESSMENT AND FOLLOW-UP

1. Check each of the following, which describe the way you usually approach relationships.

    ___ a. I do not set up rejection situations.

    ___ b. I acknowledge and deal with the pain of rejection.

    ___ c. I tune in to my body's reaction to rejection.

    ___ d. I stop the mental tape recorder.

    ___ e. I get affirmation when I need it.

    ___ f. I can determine what was actually rejected.

    ___ g. I use coping skills effectively.

    ___ h. I discard unrealistic expectations.

    ___ i. I make contact without expectations.

LIVE BEYOND REJECTION

___ j. I recognize rejection isn't always my problem.

___ k. I hurt but am not devastated by minor rejections.

___ l. I believe God wants the best for me, including my relationships.

___ m. I know that there are many rejections that are inescapable in life.

___ **Total points for a–m**

Scoring for A–M

If you checked 1–4, you need to develop better coping skills.

If you checked 5–8, you cope well sometimes, but could improve your skills.

If you checked 9–13, you have good coping skills for dealing with potential rejections.

2. Check each of the following, which describe the way you usually respond to a rejection experience.

___ n. I perceive rejection even when it isn't there.

___ o. I reject others first because they won't like me.

___ p. I reject others first because I won't like them.

___ q. I reject myself before others reject me.

___ r. I become immobilized.

___ s. I become egocentric.

___ t. I hold negative feelings inside.

___ u. I keep people at arm's length.

___ v. I sabotage relationships.

___ **Total points for n–v**

Scoring for N–V

If you checked 1–3, you do not act out of fear or use a lot of defense mechanisms.

If you checked 4–7, you sometimes set yourself up for additional rejections and need to develop better ways to respond.

If you checked 8–9, you court rejection and probably

LEARN TO RISK

frequently find it. You need to focus on learning to cope with rejection.

3. Write a letter (which you won't mail) to someone who has rejected you. Share your feelings. Talk about what you miss most from the relationship. Tell what you appreciate about him or her. Say that you will forgive the rejection. Save the letter for when you need to remind yourself that you have forgiven that person.

4. In your journal, make a list of ways you set yourself up for rejection. Identify ways to change these habits.

5. Make a cassette tape of your favorite songs or choruses to play when you are feeling sad and need some encouragement.

6. Identify several projects you would like to do someday. Obtain and gather together all of the materials you would need for each one. The next time you are feeling down, go to work on one of these projects.

✔ GROUP INTERACTION

1. **Discussion.** Use the following discussion starters to get everyone involved in the discussion. Work in groups of 5–10, giving each person a chance to complete the first statement before the group moves on to the next one. If a person is uncomfortable sharing, that person may pass.

   a. I feel rejected when. . . .

   b. I've been rejected often because. . . .

   c. One way I set myself up to be rejected is. . . .

   d. I've found I can overcome my feelings of rejection, if I. . . .

   e. My supportive network includes. . . .

   f. I turn to my support network when. . . .

   g. I have built affirmation into my life by. . . .

   h. When I feel depressed, I. . . .

   i. My experiences with reaching out to people have been good (bad) because. . . .

j. You can support me this week by praying that God will help me. . . .

2. **Graph.** Draw a graph of your life, showing the highs and lows of the last five years. On the vertical line place the words "very low" at the bottom and "very good" at the top, with words that indicate varying degrees in between. On the horizontal line, from left to right, place the dates of the last five years. After drawing the graph, identify and date specific high and low points. Share your graphs with each other and comment on how much you've survived and experienced.

3. **Role Play.** Describe on a piece of paper a rejection experience with which you have difficulty coping. Put the slips of paper in a box. In groups of two, draw a slip of paper and act out the situation. Then exchange slips of paper and have another pair act out the same situation.

4. **Book Reports.** Share about a helpful book you have read in the last month. If possible, prepare for this exercise ahead of time so that you can take the book to the group, giving you a chance to show the book to others or quote from it.

3
Let Go of the Past

I spent several of my growing-up years in the jungles of Brazil, where my parents were missionaries to a tribe of Chavante Indians. It was exciting, fun, and challenging. When I was fourteen, we returned to the States, and I discovered that I didn't really fit in with the other teenagers. I didn't know about television, radio, popular music, parties, games, or how to do the hula hoop. I was an oddball, except for my experiences in Brazil. Those made me unique. Who else could speak two other languages? Who else could boast of swimming in a river while Indians dragged a twenty-one-foot anaconda snake out of the water only four feet away? Who else had eaten monkey, alligator, and tapir? My past made me special, and I found that whenever I met someone new, I somehow worked into the initial conversation that I had grown up in the jungle. People were almost always interested, and I felt liked and appreciated.

It was years before I decided that I was more than a person who had grown up in the jungle. I had to move beyond my past. It was hard. My life in the States held no adventure compared to my life in the jungle. My self-concept was so rooted in the past that even the thought of not telling people about my life in Brazil was scary. What would I talk about? Who was I?

It's hard to let go of the past, whether it's a past identity, past relationship, past pain, past victory, or past failure. It's especially hard to let go of the past if it involves a romantic relationship. When someone special walks out of our lives with no intention of returning, we experience rejection of the first degree.

When we feel the pain of the past, we have two alternatives: either we can hold on to the pain as long as possible, or we can let go and get on with our lives. However, we act as if we had a third alternative: to return to life as it was before the painful experience. We spend a lot of time looking back with longing, wishing that life could be different.

THOSE WERE THE DAYS

Most of us do look back to the past, remembering what fun we had and how great we felt. Sometimes we look back because the present is difficult or because we are afraid of what the future might bring.

In the midst of incredible pain, the Old Testament Job looked back. "Oh, for the years gone by when God took care of me, when he lighted the way before me and I walked safely through the darkness; yes, in my early years, when the friendship of God was felt in my home; when the Almighty was still with me and my children were around me; when my projects prospered and even the rock poured out streams of olive oil to me. Those were the days."[1]

Another Old Testament story tells of a woman who looked back and lost her life.[2] The angels had told Lot to leave the city with his family to avoid the impending destruction. They warned him, "Run for your life! Don't look back, and don't stop anywhere in the plain! Flee to the mountains or you will be swept away!" The message is clear: leave and don't look back. But Lot's wife couldn't do it. She turned around and looked back. And she was turned into a pillar of lava ash.

On a trip to Europe a few years ago I visited the site of ancient Pompeii. When Vesuvius erupted, many people tried to escape. Some made it, but others didn't. The museums display molds of people who got caught in the lava flow, buried in ashes. One such person appears to have been trampled down in the rush for he is lying on his stomach, with one hand reaching out as if in anger, an expression of hopelessness on his face. I wonder what expression was on Lot's wife's face? The New Testament instructs us to remember

Lot's wife.[3] She has a lesson for us. Those who look back will be forever rooted in the past and will *lose their lives* because they refuse to live in the present or face the future. We may not die physically, but we can die emotionally, socially, and spiritually by living in the past rather than in the today God has given us.

Is the memory of the past worth giving up your whole life for? You can't curl up with a memory!

The apostle Paul gives us good advice: "I don't say that I have it all together or that I understand it all, but one thing I have learned to do: forget the things that are behind me and look forward to what is ahead and stretch forward toward the promise of what God has in store for me."[4] Paul's attitude reflects abundant living. He's not caught up in the past or bound by it. Instead, he *chooses* to look forward in faith to what God will lead him into. He's not fearful; he's expectant. He's not crippled by the past; he's confident of the God who will lead him into the future.

LETTING GO IS HARD

Why is it so hard to let go of the past? One reason is because we are afraid the future will not be as good as the past. A once-popular song captured this feeling, "If I Can't Have You, I Don't Want Nobody Else!" So instead of getting on with life, we keep looking back, hanging on to the memory of what we had.

A second reason we don't let go of the past is because we have been trapped by a habit or a memory. A certain circus bear spent his life in a twelve-foot cage, traveling around Europe, having people yell and try to make him move or growl. When the bear grew too old to be in the circus, a rich benefactor made a special outdoor home for the bear at a zoo. The new home was everything a bear could want, including a lot of privacy. But there was a problem. At first the bear wouldn't budge out of the cage. The zoo keepers coaxed him with food, prodded him with sticks, and finally had to build a fire in the rear of the cage to get the bear to come out. And when he did, he spent the next few months pacing back and forth, twelve feet at a time. The cage was gone, but he was still

LET GO OF THE PAST

trapped by his memory of the past. He died several months later.

I know people like that bear. The past is over and done with, but they are still trapped by that past—by twelve-foot ruts.

Randall took a new job and discovered that he didn't have the skills necessary for what he was expected to do. He failed. Embarrassed, he returned to his old position and never again tried something different. And the pain of that failure is as acute today as it was fifteen years ago when the incident occurred.

Katy's father rejected her when she was five years old. At thirty-five she still does not trust men.

Jeff's wife left him for his best friend. His response to the double betrayal is not to let anyone else get close enough to hurt him again.

Sandy still tells the story of her divorce to anyone who will listen. She counts on the sympathy of the listeners, considering it the only affirmation she knows how to get. Rehearsing and reliving her pain has kept it alive for the nine years since her divorce.

How sad to think of people stuck in their twelve-foot ruts, unable to see that the cage is gone. How sad to see them stuck in the past, unable to live today or look forward to tomorrow.

But I think the basic reason we don't let go of the past is that there is always a payoff for hanging on. The doctor's ex-wife received sympathy when she told her sad story to new acquaintances. And she was protected from the pain of another rejection because she never dared risk reaching out again.

Sometimes the payoff is that we allow ourselves to justify hanging on to our anger as the "injured innocent party" instead of having to face the fact that we need to forgive and move on. Sometimes the payoffs are the wonderful memories of good feelings we reexperience as we dwell on and relive the good times we used to have.

Each of us finds our own reasons for clinging to the past instead of eagerly reaching for the present. And each of us pays a personal price for doing so.

PAYING THE PRICE FOR HANGING ON TO THE PAST

When we choose to hang on to the past, we pay a price. We choose stagnation rather than personal growth. We choose the twelve-foot cage rather than a world of new relationships, skills, and challenges. Until we let go of the past, we are not free to grow. We are imprisoned.

I once knew a woman who enjoyed a luxurious lifestyle provided by her husband, a wealthy doctor. However, when he walked out of her life and got a divorce, her lifestyle was drastically changed. She had to get a job, move to a tiny apartment, and carefully watch her spending. Although she had been divorced six years when I met her, she had tears in her eyes when she shared that what she wanted most in life was to be married to a doctor and have a luxurious lifestyle again. She freely admitted that she missed the lifestyle more than she did a husband. She dreamed to return to the past. While I was touched by her deep sadness and hopelessness, I was reminded of Lot's wife. This woman had indeed lost at least six years of her life by looking back.

Once I was stuck in a rut like this one. All of my life I had wanted to write, had felt driven to write. I had tried everything and had a few things published, a couple of books, some curriculum materials, and random articles. Then I became a managing editor of a small, new magazine. Because it involved writing and editing, I was thrilled. I worked hard—writing letters, licking envelopes, planning issues, proofreading, pasting up the layouts, labeling magazines, sorting thousands of letters by zip codes, and designing marketing strategies. Sure it was fun, but I had little spare time for anything else, especially writing!

Through the years I became very attached to the magazine. Then when the owners sold the magazine to another group, I was suddenly left without my "baby." It was very tough for me to let go.

In retrospect, I wonder just how many years of my life I would have spent doing dozens of time-consuming tasks that had little to do with writing! As long as I was caught up in the duties of being the managing editor, I wasn't reaching my goals of writing books. But at the time, all I saw was what I was losing, not what I was gaining. Had I not let go of the magazine, I would not have had the opportunity to do what I really wanted to do. Unfortunately, we often can't make those judgments at the time of a loss. We usually are in too much pain to start looking for the silver lining of the cloud.

Suzanne has so much to offer a new relationship, but she refuses even to go to coffee with a man because she chooses to believe that all men are turkeys. One man has hurt her, so she assumes all men will do the same. In hanging on to her past hurt, Suzanne chooses a twelve-foot cage. She pays the price. And the price she pays is anger, bitterness, and joylessness.

If we hang on to the past, we may pay the price in anxiety, stress, pain, lost opportunities, desire for revenge, worthlessness, hopelessness, and despair. When we cling to unproductive memories or fantasies, we lack the energy and time for productive endeavors. Our self-image suffers because we focus on rejection, failure, and loss. We eventually may lose some of our friends, who may begin to tire of our constant living in the past. When we hang on to the past, we are not free to grow, to accomplish our goals.

Are the payoffs worth the price?

We can choose another way. We don't have to hang on to the past. We can choose a fuller life of growth and new relationships. Once again, the apostle Paul gives us good advice: "Get rid of all bitterness, rage and anger, brawling and slander, along with every form of malice."[5] Get rid of it. Let it go! Choose to let go of whatever is holding you back from experiencing the full scope of what God has planned for you. Choose the better way.

LET IT GO

Imagine runners preparing for a 440-meter footrace. Two of the runners show up looking as if they are going on a backpacking trip. The coach walks over to the two and asks why they have equipment on their backs. The runners respond that they are just taking things they might need for the race: rain gear, water, first-aid kit, extra shoes, and a compass.

Trying not to lose his temper, the coach explains that they are going to run only a few hundred meters and that he

LEARN TO RISK

has already made provisions in case of any emergency. He tells them to put down their gear and get in the race.

One runner drops his gear and walks to the starting line. The other stubbornly walks to the starting line with his gear on his back. The first runner finishes the race while the other is quickly left behind and finally drops out altogether, muttering, "Well, at least I was prepared!"

We all face the same choices the runners had. We can let go of unproductive attitudes, fears, and behaviors, or we can continue to keep them around because we might "need" them someday! The writer of Hebrews says, "Let us strip off anything that slows us down or holds us back, especially those sins that wrap themselves so tightly around our feet and trip us up; and let us run with patience the particular race that God has set before us."[6]

In order to live an abundant life, we must be willing to let go of past pain, present bitterness, impossible fantasies, memories that immobilize us, and imaginary fears. Frank needs to let go of his unhealthy behavior patterns. Laverne needs to let go of her resentment toward her ex-husband. Candy needs to let go of her fear of failure. Shawn needs to let go of her fantasy of marrying a minister. Earl needs to let go of his fear of change. Whatever is holding us back, we need to be willing to let it go and reach for life.

HOLD ON TO THE LESSONS

We are who we are because of where we have been and what we have learned along the way. In letting go of the past, we shouldn't let go of the lessons we learned through our experiences.

We've all said, "If only I had done this. . . ." Well, next time, do it! Learn from what you have experienced and add to your skills in the next experience.

Kent and Julie dated for three years. During their evenings together, Kent dominated their conversations with his strong opinions and judgments. Whenever Julie expressed an opinion, he quickly shot it down with a verbal barrage. Finally Julie couldn't take it anymore. She left Kent, after telling him why, and began to date another person.

Kent had a choice. He could become bitter about Julie's decision, or he could choose to learn from his mistakes and grow from them. He decided he would hold on to the lesson he learned. He now is dating Renee. He tries to listen more sensitively to her and encourages her to express her ideas. He has talked with her about his tendency to dominate other people and has asked her to let him know when she feels he is dominating her.

Kent made the right choices. He let go of the bitterness of losing Julie, but he held on to the lesson he learned from their relationship. Kent found the path to a fuller, richer relationship.

RISKS OF LETTING GO

For several months Jim had been wallowing in the bitterness of a lost relationship. His relationship to Lynn had been a destructive one, and he had decided to call it quits. The few weeks after he withdrew from the relationship were harder than he had imagined they would be. Jim felt unprotected, vulnerable, emotionally naked, and needy. He was uncomfortable and didn't know how to fill his time because he didn't have the other person to do things with. At times his worst fears were realized: he felt alone and unloved because he wasn't in a relationship.

Jim felt the price of letting go.

But it wasn't long before Jim found positive results too. He received a lot of affirmation from those who loved and cared about him. He found that he had the freedom to develop new skills and try new activities. After attending personal-growth classes and learning to share his feelings, he found joy in making new friends. He set new goals and started pursuing them successfully. He had time, energy, and a desire to live the abundant life.

Jim experienced the payoffs of letting go.

TRUST GOD

Remember that when we let go of the past, we must choose to embrace the present and the future. As Christians we

LEARN TO RISK

can look to the future with confidence because God promises to be with us. If we need help remembering his promises to us, we can look to his Word for assurance:

- "Forget the former things; do not dwell on the past. See, I am doing a new thing! Now it springs up; do you not perceive it?"[7]
- "Ask and it will be given to you; seek and you will find; knock and the door will be opened to you. For everyone who asks receives; he who seeks finds; and to him who knocks, the door will be opened. Which of you, if your son asks for bread, will give him a stone? Or if he asks for a fish, will give him a snake? If you, then, though you are evil, know how to give good gifts to your children, how much more will your Father in heaven give good gifts to those who ask him!"[8]

So why aren't we asking? Or are we asking and not receiving? Some New Testament verses give us some clues: "You want something but don't get it.... You do not have, because you do not ask God. When you ask, you do not receive, because you ask with the wrong motives, that you may spend what you get on your own pleasures."[9] If God is willing to give us good things, we need to trust his judgment if he is not giving us what we ask for. Perhaps it isn't for our own good. I'll never forget the time my one-year-old son wanted the big knife I was using to cut up meat. He demanded. He yelled. He reached. Big tears rolled down his cheeks as he sobbed because I was being so mean to him. I wonder if I sometimes look that way to God when I plead and plead for something that he knows isn't good for me!

Go to God for comfort. Consider these promises:

- "When you pass through the waters, I will be with you; and when you pass through the rivers, they will not sweep over you. When you walk through the fire, you will not be burned; the flames will not set you ablaze."[10]
- "To all who mourn ... [God] will give: beauty for ashes; joy instead of mourning; praise instead of heaviness."[11]

LET GO OF THE PAST

- "Those who sow tears shall reap joy."[12]

We need to claim those promises, or else we can be stuck in the past forever.

If you read about the rebuilding of the temple at Jerusalem in the book of Ezra, you will note that when the foundation was laid, the people gathered around and celebrated with shouts of joy. But some of the older men and priests looked at the modest beginnings and remembered the splendor of Solomon's temple. There was no comparison! They knew that this little temple would never be like Solomon's. They would never have such a wonderful temple again. What a letdown! Instead of rejoicing that after years of being in captivity they were now free in their own land and were building a temple to worship God, they saw only that it wasn't what they once had.

Instead of celebrating with the others, these disappointed people wept loudly. The writer tells us that *the people outside couldn't hear the shout of joy because of the loud weeping!*[13]

What the mourners didn't know was that in spite of its lack of splendor, the new temple would have an even greater significance in Jewish history than even Solomon's temple in all its glory!

Don't let the daily shouts of joy in your life be drowned out by the sound of your weeping for the past. Take the first steps toward becoming healed.

Learn to love the Lord with your *whole* (entire) heart, so you can love others with your *whole* (healed) heart. Let go.

✔ SELF-ASSESSMENT AND FOLLOW-UP

1. Mark with an X those questions you would answer with a yes.

    Do you cling?

    ___ Do you keep every letter you ever received?

    ___ Do you save all old Christmas cards and spend time fretting over people who don't call you?

LEARN TO RISK

___ Do you write long letters to people who don't write back?

___ Do you always make the contacts with friends?

___ Do you have dozens of boxes of mementos from as far back as grade school?

___ Do you keep inviting to your house people who always say no?

___ Do you carry grudges?

___ Do you remember disappointments and spend a lot of time trying to avoid more?

___ Do you live painfully in the past?

Do you let go?

___ Do you toss most letters after reading them?

___ Do you donate Christmas cards to worthy causes, such as community crafts?

___ Do you move people from the letter list to the Christmas-card list when they never answer your letters?

___ Do you keep making contact only when the responsibility is shared?

___ Do you toss out or give away things you don't use frequently?

___ Do you stop inviting people to your home after several "no" responses?

___ Do you forgive easily?

___ Do you figure you can't have everything and just go on?

___ Do you live joyfully in the now?

2. Make a poster of the things, experiences, or people you have difficulty letting go of. You might make drawings or use torn-out magazine pictures to illustrate the poster. Hang the poster in your bedroom so you can resolve each morning and evening to let go.

3. Make a list of unproductive memories you cling to. Then calculate what it costs you not to let go. Review the lists

LET GO OF THE PAST

and consider whether or not you want to make new choices.

4. Write a poem about the "shouts of joy" God has brought into your life in the last month.

5. Spread a few shouts of joy into the lives of three friends this week. Send flowers or cards, call them up, go out to lunch together, or plan little surprises for them.

✔ GROUP INTERACTION

1. **Discussion.** Use the following discussion starters to get everyone involved in the discussion. Work in groups of 5–10, giving each person a chance to complete the first statement before the group moves on to the next one. If a person is uncomfortable sharing, that person may pass.

   a. I can't seem to let go of. . . .

   b. The reason I hold on to past pain is. . . .

   c. If I were to let go of _____, I think that. . . .

   d. Someone who is holding on to me is. . . .

   e. Letting go of the past is hard because. . . .

   f. I'd like to return to the time when. . . .

   g. When I look ahead, I'm most afraid of. . . .

   h. I have successfully let go of. . . .

   i. What helped me let go in that instance was. . . .

   j. What I learned about letting go from that experience was. . . .

2. **Character Exploration.** Do a Scripture search and find stories of biblical characters who didn't let go of the past. What were the consequences? How do these stories relate to your experiences in today's world?

3. **Scripture Search.** Make a list of Bible verses that would encourage someone who needs to let go of the past (either good memories or remembered pain). Share your list with other group members.

4
Forgive the Pain

One of the first steps in letting go of the past is forgiving the pain of past hurts. If we look inside us, many of us can find harbored pain—moments of betrayal, disappointment, unwarranted criticism, and unacknowledged sacrifice. I do. In fact, most of us have a mental art gallery where we have hung framed pictures of our pain at its worst. Each time we are hurt again, we tend to go to our gallery and review other pictures of similar pain. We increase our pain by telling ourselves that we were hurt before, and we will be hurt again.

The gospel of Matthew tells us that when it comes to trouble, "each day has enough trouble of its own."[1] Perhaps we need to remember that verse and not look back and add past pain to the present one! Taking each situation as it comes and dealing with just one situation is easier than always dredging up past experiences and adding them to today's. And when it comes to pain, there's plenty to deal with, one situation at a time.

Burt's new boss took an instant dislike to him the moment they met. For the last six years Burt has done nothing right in the boss's eyes. Unfair? Yes. But Burt keeps hoping that someday his boss will recognize his talent.

Susan's husband left her for the woman next door. Susan came home one day and found that her husband not only had moved out but also had taken most of the furniture, wall hangings, and yard tools. He cleaned out the checking account and closed their joint savings account. She felt betrayed, hurt, and angry! That was four years ago. Susan has yet to trust another person.

Kristy's uncle raped her when she was ten, and forced her to have sex with him for the next five years. She has grown up into a lovely woman of thirty-five, but she can't stand for anyone to touch her. She doesn't even like to shake hands.

In a fit of anger, Kurt's father called him several unpleasant names and finished with "You'll never amount to anything! I'm sorry that you are my son!" Kurt hasn't seen his father in years.

Each of us has been hurt, most of us very deeply. But as long as we hang on to the pain, we are sacrificing the joy that today has to offer. We must learn to let go and forgive the pain in order to get on with our lives. That's easy to say, but hard to do!

PAST-DUE ACCOUNTS

Glen is the business manager of a small company. At the end of each fiscal year, Glen reviews the company's accounts and closes out the books. Among other things, he notes delinquent accounts—credit accounts that are past due.

Glen says that in many ways his company loses money on credit accounts: some of the company's assets are tied up in credit accounts, and it takes lots of accounting hours to maintain the accounts and to follow up on delinquent ones. Glen says that the interest charged on the past-due accounts doesn't always cover these costs.

Eventually, when Glen has exhausted every avenue to collect on delinquent accounts, the company writes them off as "bad debts." It's no longer worth the time and energy to maintain the past-due accounts.

We keep accounts also. Ours are very complicated books. They would drive an accountant mad! Some of our account pages are titled:

People not to trust
People who have let me down
People who owe me a favor or money
People who have hurt me

LEARN TO RISK

People who have hurt my friends

We tend to consider most of these accounts past due and delinquent. Yet we fail to close the books or treat them as "bad debts" and write them off. Instead, we expend vast amounts of energy maintaining the accounts, energy we could be devoting to other, more positive pursuits.

Carrying a lot of bad debts on the books for a long period of time is not healthy for a business. And it's not healthy for us as human beings. We need to "forgive our debtors" and close the books on the past.[2]

The New Testament gives us guidelines about how to deal with our past hurts and how to forgive: "If you are angry, be sure that it is not out of wounded pride or bad temper. Never go to bed angry—don't give the devil that sort of foothold.... Let there be no more resentment, no more anger or temper, no more violent self-assertiveness, no more slander and no more malicious remarks. Be kind to each other, be understanding. Be as ready to forgive others as God for Christ's sake has forgiven you."[3]

We read that and sometimes say "Yes, Lord, but you don't understand. I'm not big enough to forgive! There's too much to forgive! He's not even sorry! She doesn't deserve to be forgiven!" And we let it go at that. Maybe we can learn some lessons from the Old Testament character Joseph.[4]

JOSEPH'S PAST-DUE ACCOUNTS

Joseph experienced many hurts in his life, from his family, employers, and friends. As a result, he lived with several past-due accounts.

Account 1: Joseph's Brothers

At seventeen, Joseph had a special status at home. He was loved by his father, was given a unique coat of many colors, had loads of self-assurance, and was envied by his brothers. At their first opportunity, his brothers took his coat, threw him into a pit, later pulled him out, and sold him as a slave to a caravan headed for Egypt. On account of his brothers, Joseph was rejected, lost his family, lost his status, had to learn a new language, and had to make a new life in a strange land. His brothers left him with a sizable account.

Account 2: Potiphar and His Wife

In Egypt, Joseph came to work for Potiphar, the captain of the guard for the ruling Pharaoh. Joseph performed so well and proved his worth so quickly that soon he was placed in charge of everything Potiphar owned. The Lord blessed Joseph, and Potiphar trusted him. Once again Joseph had a special status. But then Potiphar's wife sexually harassed him and then cried "rape" when he wouldn't play along with her. Because Potiphar believed his wife's story, he stripped Joseph of all his authority and threw him into prison. Once again Joseph lost everything: his status, his new possessions, his place in his "family."

Account 3: The Chief Cupbearer

Joseph's leadership abilities were recognized even in prison. He soon earned the respect of the prison keeper and was put in charge of the other prisoners. One day Joseph interpreted a dream for two of the prisoners, Pharaoh's chief cupbearer and chief baker. The chief cupbearer, whose dream predicted that he would be restored to his position with the Pharaoh, was so grateful that he promised that as soon as he was free, he would try to get Joseph released. But the cupbearer forgot Joseph.

Eventually Joseph was released from prison and honored by the Pharaoh. He built a new life, for the third time. He was made second in command in all of Egypt. He was special! He was respected. He had a new status and a new family. He eventually married and had two sons. At the birth of his first son, Joseph took stock of his life. Feeling very grateful to God, he named the boy Manasseh (which means "forgetting") because he said, "God has made me forget all my trouble and all my father's household."[5]

But a few years later Joseph's brothers came to Egypt to buy food because of a famine. When Joseph saw them, he forgot to forget. Instead, he remembered that his brothers had a past-due account on the books. Realizing that his brothers didn't recognize him, Joseph decided to make them suffer a bit.

Even though he was generous with them and provided for them, he made life hard for them. Finally Joseph decided to forgive his brothers. When he revealed his identity to them, they kissed each other and cried for joy. After that, the Bible says, "they talked." Full communion and communication is possible after true forgiveness.

It was after Joseph had truly forgiven the pain of the past that he was able to fulfill one of the most important purposes in his life: to save the Jewish nation from extinction because of the famine. God had blessed Joseph all along, but this special honor came after he was willing to reach out to forgive those who had hurt him. In fact, Joseph not only forgave them and helped them, but he also later honored them as he made them rulers over Pharaoh's cattle!

What past-due accounts do you maintain? How much energy do you spend keeping those accounts open? Are you ready to consider letting go and forgiving the pain, to find out if there is a higher blessing for your life just waiting for you? Some days I find that I'm ready to forgive, and some days I find it impossible to move on. I get stuck trying to do it my way instead of God's way.

MY WAY OR GOD'S WAY?

"Forgiving doesn't come easy!" Tammy argues, and she is right. Forgiving is not a natural instinct. What is natural is to try to protect ourselves and our rights. If we touch a hot stove and get burned, we're not too eager to touch it again. If someone betrays a trust, we don't rush to trust again. Tammy continues, "But I'm the one who was wronged. Why should I go that extra mile and forgive him?"

I know how she feels. Over the years I too have wrestled with the pain of rejection, betrayal, and failed expectations. I too was not eager to forgive.

But forgiving is God's way. His Word often instructs us to forgive the people who have hurt us deeply. He not only wants us to forgive, but he want us to forgive freely.

Forgiving is God's way not only because he tells us to forgive, but also because that's the way he treats us. Even though we have hurt him deeply, he forgives us. He is the God "who forgives *all* [our] sins."⁶ And he paid a personal price in order to forgive us: his son, Jesus Christ, died to pay the penalty for the hurts we have caused him and other people.

Once, when someone had wronged me and the pain was too much to bear, I decided I needed to learn more about forgiveness. Through my reading I found this statement, which meant a lot to me: *"Forgiveness is not a receipt for a payment in full!"* It opened a window through which I could see the possibilities of forgiving.

Think about it. Real forgiveness does not demand payment in full, restitution. If the debt is "paid," then there is no forgiving left to do! Basically physical restitution may restore something we have lost (money, a favorite record, a vase), but there is no way another person can effect emotional restitution. That must come from within. We are the only ones who can rebuild and restore emotional wholeness, and the first step in the restoration is forgiveness.

Also, as we begin to forgive, we should not try to *understand* the other person and his or her motives. Instead, we should try to *be understanding* and accepting. If we are trying to understand, we set up ourselves as judges. We will forgive if we deem their excuses or their motives to be acceptable, and we will not forgive if we cannot "understand" why they did what they did! However, if we work at being understanding, we operate from the position that people are doing the best they can. If they had the ability to cope another way, they would do so.

Carol tries to understand. When her friend was late for dinner, she forgave him because he had a flat tire on the way. But if he had been late because he had watched the last quarter of the football game before driving to her house, Carol might not have forgiven him.

Dennis, on the other hand, tries to be understanding. When people are late for dinner at his house, he gives them the benefit of the doubt and assumes that they had a good reason, whatever it was.

When I was struggling to forgive a serious hurt in my own life, I learned about forgiveness through this analogy. When parents bring home a new baby from the hospital, they are excited. But within hours of coming home, the baby will wet his or her diaper and have to be changed. Although few of us would rate this as one of life's greatest pleasures, most of us recognize that babies cope with their physical needs the best way they can. A one-week-old baby can't speak up and ask to use the restroom. Babies wet their diapers, and in the process sometimes they ruin someone's expensive silk shirt or dress.

But most of us wouldn't throw the baby into the crib and scream angrily, "How could you do this to me after all I've done for you!" There's nothing to get angry about. The baby is doing the best he or she can.

And we don't change the diaper and then tell the baby seriously, "I forgive you for wetting your diaper." There's nothing to forgive! How do you fault someone for doing the best he or she can?

We would not be as understanding of a wet diaper if the baby were sixteen years old, because we expect that by then the child would have learned to cope differently with bodily needs. However, sometimes babies don't mature at the normal rate. They are developmentally disabled. So they don't walk at ten months or talk at two years. They may stay at a one-year developmental level even though they are six or sixteen years old. But we don't fault them for not performing at their chronological age level because we understand that they haven't developed those skills yet. So instead of being angry with these developmentally disabled people for not being more skilled than they are, we care for them and teach them the skills we want them to learn. We usually have a right attitude in such instances.

I think this principle applies to all of us. We all develop on several levels: physical, emotional, social, relational, intellectual, and spiritual. It would be nice, I think, if we developed regularly at a standard rate of speed so that when we are twelve, we are at a certain set point on each of those levels and when we are twenty we are at the twenty-year point. Unfortunately we develop at our own rates of speed and on different levels at different times. So no one truly can predict where we are in our developmental process at any given time unless they know us well enough to speak from experience.

Even though we don't know where other people are in their development, we usually act as if they are supposed to be at a certain place on each of the levels. In other words, we expect every adult we meet to be honest, caring, trustworthy, ready for a commitment to a good relationship, gentle, accepting, self-confident, and on and on. In essence we say, if a person is over twenty-five (for example), he or she can be expected to behave in a certain way. But that's not reality!

None of us is fully mature or perfect. We are developing. We are becoming. Some of us develop faster than others; some grow up much slower than we would wish. But what if instead of faulting people, we looked beyond the behavior and saw the need for being loved and accepted, and we responded to that need?

Is James selfish because he is afraid that if he doesn't look out for himself, no one else will?

Is Katy critical because she is so insecure that she can't see anyone else as better than she is?

Does Bill reject others because he is afraid that no one will accept him and doesn't want to risk rejection?

Is Janie unfaithful because she hasn't learned how to make a commitment and is afraid of trusting one person totally?

Whatever the reason for the way we act, we all have basic needs. We want to be loved and accepted by those who are important in our lives. We want people to trust us. We want to be given the benefit of the doubt. If we all want that, why don't we offer that to each other?

Surely, we would like to see our friends further along in their development in some areas, but they are doing the best they can. We need to be understanding. We need to acknowledge where they are in their development and accept that.

I'm sure that God looks at me and wishes I were further along than I am in my development toward being conformed to the image of Christ. But I also know he is understanding. He knows I'm growing as fast as I can, and he celebrates each new step I take.

Ideally, I would like to come to the point of maturity in my life where I could always look past the other person's offensive behavior to his needs and be neither hurt nor angry. But I have yet to reach that point in my life. We live in a world where people are going to let us down and hurt us. All of us must be willing to forgive, remembering that we all develop and grow according to our own unique timetables. We must choose to let go of the pain and forgive.

Again I think of the baby illustration. When that nine- or ten-month-old baby begins to stand alone and tries to take the first step, we get ready to celebrate. We find the camera and keep it handy as we follow the baby from room to room, waiting to catch that first step on film. When we do, we race to the phone and call Mom to tell her the baby is walking! We don't criticize those first tentative steps. We don't berate the baby for falling down after two steps. We don't blame the child for crawling for a few minutes before trying to walk again! We don't criticize. We celebrate.

If only we could treat our adult friends the same way—no criticizing tentative first tries and early failures—just celebrating each step toward a new goal, each effort made.

We don't treat our friends this way because we aren't always ready to put away our anger toward someone who fails to live up to our expectations. We often decide that we can't afford to pay the price of forgiving the other person. But if we think the cost of forgiving is high, we will find that the cost of not forgiving is even higher.

THE COST OF NOT FORGIVING

Sometimes we don't forgive because we think the personal cost is more than we can afford to pay. A friend of mine tells the story of his favorite antique rocking chair, which was broken by some careless teenagers after he had cautioned them to treat it gently. Angry and hurt, he hid the pieces of the chair in a corner of his basement. Each day during the winter months as he exercised in the basement, those pieces reminded him how angry he was at the boys who had hurt him by breaking the chair.

When spring came, my friend was able to run outside again, so he no longer had to look at the broken pieces. One day as he ran, he noticed a furniture repair place. Each day as he ran past that shop, he would relive his anger, certain that he could never afford to pay to have his rocker repaired.

Finally in an effort to get past his pain, my friend entered the store to find out just how much it would cost to have his chair repaired. He was shocked to discover that the cost was minimal. He immediately dashed home for the broken pieces and gave them to the shop keeper. Within days he had his chair back, almost as good as new.

Because he had assumed that he couldn't afford the cost of repair, he had gone without his favorite chair for months. My friend had suffered unnecessary pain and anger.

Sometimes we do the same with relationships. Because we think we can't afford to forgive, we sacrifice what we want most and suffer unnecessary pain and anger.

A group of single people shared together about painful experiences in their lives. Gary told his story, almost as if he was understanding for the first time just what a price he was paying for hanging on to the pain of the past. He told about how he had tried to earn his father's respect and love by working in the yard and pleasing his father. When his father arrived home from work one day, nine-year-old Gary called out to him, pleased by the good job he had done of the mowing and raking: "Look, Dad, see what I've done!"

"Well, you're not finished yet!" his dad responded and launched into a lecture about doing things right, about weeding and edging, about all the things Gary had not done. Gary got defensive and his dad became angry. Soon they were fighting. Exasperated, Gary's dad shouted at him, "If you don't shape up, you won't amount to anything in life!"

Now thirty years old, Gary still remembers vowing at that moment that he would never forgive his father and that he would prove his dad wrong. He vowed to become a better man than his father ever was. And in many ways he did.

Gary spent most of his life trying to live up to that childhood vow. He drove himself to make better grades than his dad had made, to get a job at an earlier age than his father had, and to enter a higher paying career and to get promoted more quickly than his father had. He succeeded in all of these goals, and he never forgave his father.

As Gary shared his story, the pain and sadness was evident in his whole demeanor. When he finished, the leader quietly asked, "And what has this success cost you?"

As the realization dawned, Gary responded hoarsely,

"My father. It has cost me my father. We don't have a relationship, only a competition." One of the costs of not forgiving is losing a relationship with someone we care about.

Another cost of not forgiving is that we carry a load of anger, hurt, disappointment, and fear. We tie up a lot of energy being careful around the person who has hurt us so that we won't be hurt again. We are more tentative with that person and less open and caring with him or her. We resist efforts on the other person's part to continue the relationship on its former basis.

A third consequence of not forgiving is that we run the risk of not being forgiven by our Father in heaven. The Gospels remind us that if we forgive other people's hurts against us, God will forgive us. But if we don't forgive others, God will not forgive us.[7]

The whole basis of our relationship to God is that he loved us enough to send his Son to die for us, even though we are sinners. We often aren't even sorry for our sins, and we can never make adequate restitution to God for the break in our relationship with him. Yet if we admit our sin to him and express our desire to change, he promises to forgive each daily transgression, sin, and failing. He loves us enough to forgive us always. He tells us that "if we confess our sins, he is faithful and just and will forgive us our sins and purify us from all unrighteousness."[8]

Experiencing God's healing forgiveness after we have failed is a wonderful restorative to a wounded spirit. As we grow to be more like him, we can learn to become forgiving persons toward one another.

BE FORGIVING

Lois was convinced that Henry had invited her to lunch to break off their relationship. She was relieved it was going to be settled because in the last few weeks it seemed as if he had gone out of his way to hurt her in a dozen little ways. She felt sad, but somewhat prepared, for their conversation—or so she thought.

When Henry started to share about how in the last few weeks he had been struggling with the fact that he was truly

FORGIVE THE PAIN

falling in love with her, Lois was puzzled at first. *What was there to struggle about?* she asked herself, but she listened quietly and learned why.

Intimacy was scary for Henry. Although he wanted an intimate relationship with Lois, at the same time he subconsciously was sabotaging their relationship with behaviors he instantly regretted. He wanted to make a commitment to her, but he hadn't made a conscious choice to do so.

As Lois listened to him share his struggles, she realized that, in spite of his behaviors, he truly loved her and cared about their relationship. She felt the pain begin to fade and saw the hurtful events of the last few weeks from a different perspective. Now she knew that those times had hurt him as much or even more than they had hurt her. She freely forgave him and discovered that forgiveness was what took away the pain from her memories. A sign of true forgiveness is not forgiving and forgetting, but forgiving and hurting no more.

A prominent man had an affair and as a result left the marriage in disgrace. His wife was hurt; his children, angry; his church, shocked. He lost the lady he had been seeing to another relationship, his children who refused to talk with him, and his job because of failing eyesight.

At first, his wife felt these losses were well deserved and simply the natural consequences of his faulty choices. Later, she began to feel sorry for him and even thought she could forgive him. Unknown to her, their children, one by one, began to make contact with their father.

A year and a half after the divorce, the wife's mother became ill and she flew back East to be with her. There she found a bouquet of flowers delivered that morning from her children and ex-husband. She was surprised but then shocked later when her oldest daughter called.

"Mom," the girl said hesitantly, "Dad wants you to do a favor for him. He wants you to tell Grandma he's sorry and to ask her forgiveness."

The wife knew how judgmental her mother had always been toward her former husband. She didn't want to do this favor. She told herself, *I'm the one who was hurt the most! Why do I have to obtain forgiveness for him?* But in the spirit of him who seeks God's forgiveness for us when we sin, she talked to her mother. "That's when the real forgiveness came into my own heart," she shared. "That's when my own healing began."

Forgiveness does not call for one person to assume the total responsibility for a relationship; rather both parties have a responsibility to their relationship. But just because one person is not doing his or her share doesn't give the remaining partner license to sacrifice the relationship. Care enough to forgive. Care enough to risk again. Care enough to love.

✔ SELF-ASSESSMENT AND FOLLOW-UP

1. How forgiving are you? Check which of the following statements describe your approach to problems in relationships.

   ___ I find it easy to say I'm sorry.

   ___ I try to be understanding of the other person.

   ___ I know most people are doing the best they can.

   ___ I know no one person can live up to all of my expectations.

   ___ I can be hurt and still value the person who hurt me.

   ___ If I care enough about a relationship, I'll make the first move toward reconciliation, even if I'm the one who was wronged.

   ___ I can forgive and let go of my grudge.

   ___ When a relationship is restored after a hurt, I'm willing to risk trusting that person again.

2. Make a list of all the people who have wronged you. Place an X next to those you suspect you haven't yet forgiven. Promise yourself that you will begin to work on forgiving each one.

3. Read *Caring Enough to Forgive* by David Augsburger. As you read, write in your journal at least five things that you will incorporate into your lifestyle in the next month.

4. Reflect on your own experiences. Identify ways in which you may have offended others; then take steps to make amends and to seek forgiveness.
5. In your journal, write a letter to yourself, reminding yourself that you are forgiven for your failures, mistakes, and shortcomings. Remind yourself that God forgives when we confess (1 John 1:9). Then forgive yourself.

✔ GROUP INTERACTION

1. **Discussion.** Read aloud Ephesians 4:32. Use the following discussion starters to get everyone involved. Work in groups of 5–10, giving each person a chance to respond to the first statement before the group moves on to the next one. If a person is uncomfortable sharing, that person may pass.
   a. Define forgiveness.
   b. What does it feel like to have someone forgive you?
   c. Why is it usually hard to forgive?
   d. When is it easy to forgive?
   e. Share something you are having difficulty forgiving.
   f. What would happen if you did forgive in that situation?
   g. What steps do you go through to forgive?
   h. What makes you ready to take that first step?
   i. One way I could be more forgiving this week would be to. . . .
   j. What does Ephesians 4:32 say to you about forgiveness in your life?

2. **Example.** Besides Jesus and Joseph, which biblical person best exemplifies forgiveness. Why? Discuss each person's suggestion and come to a group decision.

3. **Song.** Write a song about forgiveness, using a familiar tune. Sing it together.

5
Win Over Fear

One night when my mother, my two younger sisters, a houseguest, and I were home alone in the little village of Barra do Garcas, Brazil, we heard a loud commotion outside. A man began banging on the shutters of the living-room window and shouting harshly. He sounded either drunk or mentally ill as he threatened mayhem if we didn't open the door. Knowing that the shutter latches were flimsy and there were no glass panes or screens in the windows, we were frightened. We had no telephone, and the closest neighbors were half a block away.

We discussed a plan. One of us would have to go out the back door, circle widely around the house, hope to sneak unseen past the man, and go get the police. Considering all the potential dangers, our houseguest, Raimunda, took a firm position, "Eu nem vou, nem ficou!" ("I'm not going or staying!")

So often in life we are like Raimunda. We are immobilized in the present because of our fears or worries about what might happen in the future.

FOR FEAR

Our worries are based on our fears of what might happen. So what we actually need to face and work on are our secret fears—the ones we don't share easily.

I met an attractive man several years ago. He had a successful job, a lot of friends, and a terrific sense of humor. It was no wonder that most women who met Howard began having romantic fantasies about this unattached bachelor.

Howard and I spent a lot of time together over the course of several months and I realized that Howard was a very closed person. I wondered why. In time he began opening up, ever so slightly, ever so slowly, and I found out his secret. He was scared to death of being hurt again the way he had been by the desertion of his ex-wife. So far he hadn't been hurt because he had never allowed himself to care deeply about anyone.

Thinking about Howard and people like him I wrote:

FOR FEAR

For fear of being rejected,
 I'll stay by myself.
For fear of rebuff,
 I'll keep my mouth shut.
For fear of failing,
 I'll just not try.
For fear of your leaving,
 I'll not ask you to stay.
For fear of your not loving,
 I'll give up the pleasure of being with you.
For fear of missing you,
 I'll turn away from your touch.

But then, I find that I'm not living for me,
but for fear!

The last time I saw Howard, he was still attractive, still single, and still alone.

BUT WHAT IF ...

Each of us has a few worries (or fears) that plague us. But if we allow those fears to run our lives, we become immobilized. I once heard it said that "fear is the darkroom where we develop our negatives!" How true. If fear and our worries about those fears rule our lives, we won't ever do what we most want to do.

I was fourteen when we left the Brazilian Indian tribe with whom we had been living as missionaries. We were returning to the United States on furlough and would be gone for at least a year. (It turned out to be forever, because we never returned.) I didn't want to leave. This was my home. The Indians were my friends. I had been crying for days every time I thought about our leaving. As I said good-bye to all my friends, I remember wanting desperately to give one of the Indians a hug. He had lived in our house and had been like a brother to me. But with all of my adolescent inhibitions, I was too afraid to hug him. Consequently I just said good-bye and left with a very heavy heart.

For years I wanted that moment of decision back. I would have hugged him. But you can't turn back the clock and relive the moments.

All too often we let opportunities pass us by because we are afraid.

What If I Look Foolish?

How often have you refused to try something new and different because you were afraid you would look foolish?

Carol sits in the ski lodge while her friends are on the slopes. She is alone, not because she's afraid of breaking her leg, but because she doesn't want to look stupid while learning to ski.

Paul got a low grade in his college statistics class because he didn't want to ask "stupid" questions or admit he didn't understand.

The payoff for Carol and Paul's behavior is that they didn't look stupid. But the price is that they didn't learn either!

Have you ever felt like an outsider looking in on others having fun in life? Well, take action. Don't worry about looking foolish. Get involved.

What If Someone Disapproves?

They probably will! Not everyone is going to agree with every decision you make. There will always be people who don't believe in charity, risking, openness, loving, or sharing. So acknowledge that you may be criticized and go ahead and try something new.

What If I Get Hurt or Rejected?

It happens. To all of us.

Rick goes late to most singles' functions so he won't have to stand around alone. He feels that no one will want to talk with him so he doesn't give anyone a chance to reject him. Rick reminds me of my oldest son Jon.

When my sons were younger, they were very different when it came to physical affection. Jon would barely tolerate a ten-second hug, while Mike would jump in my lap and cuddle at the slightest excuse. At first I thought that Jon didn't want to be loved. But one day I caught him looking at Mike, who had run to his dad and was hugging him exuberantly. There was such a deep longing in Jon's eyes as he hung back in self-imposed loneliness.

I've seen adults do that too. They want to be loved so badly that they are afraid they can't handle not being loved. So they hold back. The truth is, the fear of rejection is actually often more painful than the rejection experience itself.

What If I Fail?

The bottom line is nothing ventured, nothing gained. No one likes to fail. But if you live your life afraid of failure, you may lead a very dull life. Besides if you plan well for new ventures, you can minimize the chances of a major failure.

Mark decided to go into the restaurant business. He quit his job, used his retirement fund to buy a small building, opened shop, and lost his shirt! But Mark's problem was not that he tried a new venture but that he hadn't developed a plan before he began. He hadn't researched the market, considered alternate funding sources, hired a good cook, or consulted the experts. The interesting thing about Mark is that he still wants to be in the restaurant business. He got his old job back and is now working on a five-year plan to try again—this time wisely.

So you fail a few times! So what? Learn from the mistakes. Learn to fail without being a failure!

LEARN TO RISK

DON'T BE A WORRYWART

Can you name one positive thing that has been accomplished by worry? I can't. People who have a lot of fears spend a lot of time worrying about what would happen if the things they fear were to happen. But worrying doesn't change what is going to happen, nor does it prepare you for the future. So since it's not a worthwhile endeavor, why do we invest time worrying? Here are some reasons.

We think worry proves we care. Darla firmly believes that worrying about her children and friends proves that she cares about them. The truth is, she worries them to death, just checking on them!

Worry keeps us from unpleasant chores. Keith is so worried about losing his job that he can't clean house, do laundry, work in the yard, or help a friend clean his garage. Instead, he sits in his kitchen with endless cups of coffee, worrying about his future.

We think worry is a good excuse to indulge. Hal gets worried and goes shopping to get his mind off his troubles. One particularly stressful month, he ran up over $1,000 in charge accounts. Nancy eats chocolate whenever she is worried. She says it makes her feel better.

Worry gets us attention. Many friends will go out of their way to comfort us and to sympathize when we are worried. And should we actually become ill from excessive worry, we'll get even more attention from those who love us.

Worry protects us from risks. George doesn't try new things because he worries about failing. Janis doesn't risk reaching out because she worries about being rejected.

With all of these payoffs, it isn't surprising that at some time or another most of us are tempted to indulge in worrying. We worry about almost everything:

    our children
    our health
    our finances
    our jobs
    our friends
    the economy
    possible war

death
accidents
the future
possible failures
the weather

And some people worry because they're waiting for the other shoe to drop. Or they worry because things are going too well. How silly can we get?

BECOME WORRY FREE

To live worry free doesn't mean we become oblivious to the harsh realities of everyday living. It does mean we have a right perspective on those realities. Being worry free means moving on, reaching out, embracing life, and facing what comes. It means that we give our fears to God, trusting him to bring about the best for us in his time.

The Old Testament character Joshua is a good example of a person who had cause to be afraid but who chose instead to have faith in God. Deuteronomy tells the story of the death of Moses, a leader who knew the Lord face to face, who did signs and wonders in the Lord's power.[1] When Moses died, the Israelites mourned for thirty days. Then the Lord said to Joshua, "Moses . . . is dead. Arise and cross the Jordan."[2] Joshua could have worried about many things.

It was a bad time. Joshua had just lost his friend, mentor, and leader. He was still mourning his losses, and God wanted him to try something risky: to lead the Israelites into enemy territory.

It was the wrong time of year. God had instructed Joshua to cross the Jordan River, but this was the season when the Jordan overflowed its banks. Joshua could have argued with God: "Why now? We've waited forty years. Why not wait a few more months?"

The priests carrying the ark had to walk into the flood. They were instructed to lead the people into the Jordan. They had to be willing to step into the waters and get their feet wet.

But Joshua wasn't afraid. He didn't say to God, "What if. . . ." He didn't worry. Instead, he trusted God to work out the details. He remembered that although Moses was dead, God was not!

Remember that even when your hopes and dreams die, God is still alive and well. He may even be saying to you, "Your dream is dead, arise and cross over to a new beginning." And when we are tempted to be afraid, we can hear the words God said to Joshua: "Be strong and courageous. Do not be terrified, do not be discouraged; for the Lord your God will be with you wherever you go."[3]

We can learn several lessons from Joshua's example.

Let God handle the big things. God is able. In fact he is the only one who is able. We can't prevent an earthquake, a recession, war, death, or even major illness. But God can! Like the priests who entered the Jordan River, be willing to take those first steps and let God handle the rest. Getting your feet wet in your "Jordan River" may be the beginning of God's miraculous involvement in your life.

Let God handle the small things. The New Testament tells us to cast all our cares on God and let him do our caring for us.[4] Our fear can't change things; God's caring can!

Let God handle the future. We can take comfort about our future, knowing that God has plans for us. "'For I know the plans that I have for you,' declares the Lord, 'plans to prosper you and not to harm you, plans to give you a hope and a future.'"[5] "Things which eye has not seen and ear has not heard, and which have not entered the heart of man, all that God has prepared for those who love Him."[6]

Thank God for today. Instead of being afraid about what today may bring, thank God for it. Learn to look at each new day and say: "This is the day that the Lord has made; [I] will rejoice and be glad in it."[7]

THREE "IF'S" THAT MAKE LIFE WORTHWHILE

In order to be free from fear, we need to abandon our "what-if," worry mentality. Instead, we need to learn three "if's" that will make life worthwhile.

If You Dare

You never know what you can accomplish until you try. (And sometimes, try again!) Suppose you put a broomstick across two chairs. How would you know if you could jump over it? You wouldn't until you tried. Suppose you miss the first time. Does that mean you can't jump that high? No. It only means that you didn't make it on the first try. Perhaps you will on the third or fourth try!

Last year I bought a fancy program for my new computer. But no matter what I tried, I couldn't get it to work. Frustrated after two days of trying, I put the program on the shelf and ignored it for a year. Last week I decided to try again. This time it worked without a hitch. You see, during the last year I've used the computer a lot and became familiar with how it works. Instructions that were like Greek to me a year ago make sense now.

Sometimes we need to try and then try again because through our losses, through our experiences, we may have learned how to do it better this time, how to be more loving, how to reach out more skillfully than before.

So dare to try!

Make decisions. Have you ever noticed how excited you can get just by making a decision to do something. You may feel confused, in a quandary, and unsure of which way to go. But as soon as you make a firm decision on what to do, you feel a surge of adrenaline inside. You feel motivated, energized! Dare to make decisions.

Make plans. My husband Ed and I take great vacations, but half of the fun of our vacations comes months before we ever leave home. We get an arm load of brochures and start dreaming. When we finally agree on a vacation, we start planning. We pick the dates. We make lists of what to take, what to see, what to do before we leave, and what questions to ask the travel agent. We truly love making plans. There's nothing like the thrill of anticipation. Made a decision? Begin to make plans!

Start. When I get ready to begin a new writing project, I clear off my desk, organize my study, and usually finish several back-burner projects before I put the first words on paper. Starting something is exciting! Kids know this. You promise to help them build a playhouse, and they want to do it *now!* Remember the last project you started and how much excitement and enthusiasm you felt? Okay, get started now!

Check your progress. We all like to know how we measure up. Kids love to measure their height to check how much they've grown. When we go on a diet, we love to weigh in to see how much we've lost. A person who works out with weights tries to lift more and more weight, making notes on his or her progress. Seeing your progress is a satisfying reward and a wonderful motivator for continued effort. In a slump? Make some significant progress toward one of your goals! It will cheer you up.

Achieve your goal. The most exciting payoff of daring to try is achieving your goal. I'll never forget the thrill of having my first book published. I grinned for days. My cheeks were actually sore from the unaccustomed exercise of smiling! It was wonderful. I had so much energy, I immediately wrote another book!

Dare to try!

If You Care

The second "if" that makes life worthwhile is *if we care.* We need to become involved with life, to reach out to others, to make a difference in our world. We can do lots of things in life, but none of them is truly worthwhile unless we have a loving, caring attitude: "If I speak with the tongues of men and of angels, but have not love, I am only a resounding noisy gong or a clanging cymbal. If I have the gift of prophecy and can fathom all mysteries and all knowledge, and if I have a faith that can move mountains, but have not love, I am nothing. If I give all I possess to the poor and surrender my body to the flames, but have not love, I gain nothing."[8]

We all need to care and be cared for, without loving friendships our lives often seem worthless and empty. I was once a guest on a secular talk show with a brilliant psychologist. He had written a best-selling book, had a very successful practice, and was a nationally known expert in his specialty. I was charmed by his wit and wisdom.

Two months later I read that he had shot himself. He had

achieved so much but had lacked the ability to form loving relationships. He chose to die rather than live his lonely existence. I was saddened.

Learn to care about life and what treasures you have. Appreciate God's handiwork in nature. Acknowledge the value of your heritage. Invest in the lives of those around you. Contribute to your church, your singles' group, missions, or the poor. Develop a special awareness and sensitivity to people in general and especially to those in your circle of friends. Become a caring, involved person, a genuine and loving ambassador for Christ.

Care!

If You Share

Everyone has a lot to share—talents, gifts, ideas, and experiences. Share your time. Get involved in your church or community. Share in a friend's struggles, dreams, goals, or plans. Half the fun of doing something is either sharing the experience at the time or sharing about it with a friend afterward.

Get involved and share.

✔ SELF-ASSESSMENT AND FOLLOW-UP

1. To what degree do worry and fear run your life? Check the statements that apply to you.

   ____ I lie awake at night worrying.

   ____ I take very few risks so I won't fail.

   ____ I let others make the first moves in relationships.

   ____ I don't try new activities so I won't look stupid if I can't do them well.

   ____ I avoid conflict at all costs.

   ____ Confronting people is almost impossible for me.

   ____ My first response to a suggestion is to list the things that might go wrong.

LEARN TO RISK

___ I really envy people who can reach out to others easily.

___ Criticism devastates me.

___ When I'm afraid, I get physically ill.

If you checked six or more of the above, you may need to get some help to deal with your worries and fear.

2. Finish this sentence at least ten different ways: I'm afraid of.... Then analyze your fears. What patterns do you see? What can you do to become free from fears?

3. Draw a picture of something you worry about at least once a week. At the bottom of the picture, write out Psalm 56:3–4. Tape the picture to your refrigerator as a daily reminder not to worry.

4. Make a list of the "what if's" that are restricting your life. Decide to let go of these and break their power over you.

5. In your journal, write a letter to God, telling him in what ways you are going to let him handle the big things, the little things, and the future. Be sure to thank him for the blessings of today.

✔ GROUP INTERACTION

1. **Discussion.** Use the following discussion starters to get everyone involved. Work in groups of 5–10, giving each person a chance to complete the first statement before the group moves on to the next one. If a person is uncomfortable sharing, that person may pass.

    a. I worry when....

    b. I can't stop worrying about....

    c. Ways I've tried to stop worrying are....

    d. In my experience, worrying is....

    e. My greatest fear is of....

    f. Letting go and letting God handle this is hard because....

    g. What I would like to dare to try is....

WIN OVER FEAR

   h. What stops me is. . . .
   i. I would like to care more by. . . .
   j. My favorite thing to share is. . . .

2. **Scripture Search.** Read the following verses and write the key concepts of each.

   Psalm 9:9–10
   Psalm 23:4
   Psalm 25:16–18
   Psalm 28:7
   Psalm 112:6–8
   Isaiah 35:4
   Isaiah 41:10, 13
   Matthew 10:28, 31
   John 14:1

   What should be the Christian's perspective of fearsome things or experiences?

3. **Poem.** Write a poem about fear or worry and the consequences of indulging in either. Share your poem.

4. **Story.** Write a contemporary story about the futility of worry.

6
Don't Wait for the "Wonderful"

"How would you describe your life in one sentence?" the group leader asked. Several people responded with statements about growing, learning, struggling, and other similar descriptive terms. Robert, however, thought for a while before he gave his answer: "I'm basically waiting for the wonderful plan to happen!" He smiled ruefully and went on to explain, "You know, we are constantly reminded that God has a wonderful plan for our lives. So far it seems that my whole life has been one big struggle after another. I'm a little tired of growing, struggling, and being strong. I'm ready for some of that 'wonderful'!"

Many of us can identify with Robert. When I consider the people with whom I have daily contact, I would say that most of them seem to be struggling in the valleys rather than living on the mountain tops. In a one week's period recently, I encountered the following:

- A female friend was going through the frustrating legalities of divorce and custody of minor children, trying to do the right thing, and wrestling with questions of what is right and what is best for the children, and does it always pay to do the right thing.
- A man called from Arizona just to tell me the painful story of his divorce after being abandoned by his wife. Feeling very alone, he needed reassurance and acceptance.
- A woman, recently betrayed by a close friend, felt that

trusting people was a foolish thing; she was withdrawing from all of her friends.
- A forty-five-year-old woman, seeing two of her friends forming new romantic relationships, began to have self-doubts and fear that she would live the rest of her life alone and lonely.
- A letter from a woman in Tennessee said that unless I could give her some reason to live, she was going to commit suicide because life had become intolerable for her.

And I wasn't having such a terrific week myself!

All of us have days when we feel less than successful and wonder secretly if this is all there is.

WHERE'S THE ABUNDANT LIFE?

God seems to have promised us something more than failure! Jesus says that he came to give us a full, abundant life.[1] The Old Testament tells us that God has good plans for our lives and that he wants to give us a future and a hope.[2] The apostle Paul says that God's will for our lives is perfect, that we can't even imagine what wonderful things God has prepared for those who love him.[3]

That all sounds good. But when we're in the midst of struggles, some of us cry with Robert, "Okay, so where's the wonderful?"

Perhaps the answer lies in the story of David.[4] I once heard a sermon that gave me a totally different perspective of David's life, especially his life after he was anointed to be king of Israel.[5] When King Saul displeased the Lord, Samuel was instructed to go to Bethlehem and anoint one of Jesse's sons as the new king. So Samuel went and called Jesse to come with his sons to the sacrifice. After the sacrifice, Jesse brought his first-born son, Eliab, to Samuel. The prophet was so impressed with tall, handsome Eliab that he was sure this was the Lord's choice. But God cautioned Samuel: "You judge a person by outward appearance, but I look at a person's thoughts and intentions."[6] Eliab was not the choice. Neither were the next six sons.

Samuel was puzzled. What was the problem? He asked Jesse if he had any more sons. Jesse also looked puzzled. "Well, there's just the youngest. But he's out in the fields keeping the sheep. You want me to bring him here?" he asked.

Samuel asked to see the boy. Jesse was amazed. David? Little David? What was Samuel thinking? Jesse shook his head. He hadn't even considered taking David to the sacrifice. David was just a child with chores to do while the men of the family took care of important business!

When David arrived, the Lord told Samuel that this was his choice for the crown. Samuel anointed David in front of the elders as God's chosen person to be the next king of Israel.

That part of the story I knew, having heard about David since I was a child myself. What I had never thought about was what happened next.

Nothing special. Nothing special happened to David after Samuel anointed him to become king. Isn't that interesting? You see, David was informed that God had a wonderful plan for his life, and then he was sent back to the fields to tend the sheep! If I were David, I might have rebelled at that. I might have said, "Wait a minute, something special just happened, right? I've just been anointed to be the next king of Israel! I have some heavy learning to do. Get someone else to watch the sheep. Send me to king school or to the palace so I can learn the royal etiquette or at least let me learn to be a soldier. I already know how to be a shepherd!"

But David went back to tending sheep. He might have had the occasional thought, "What kind of place is this for a king? No recognition, no honor, no special treatment, no training, just the same old hard work as before." But he was obedient. Surely, on some of those starry nights as he lay in the field, he must have dreamed about what it would be like when he would be the king, and he must have wondered when all this would happen.

Many of the people I meet have similar feelings. If God has such a wonderful plan for my life, then why doesn't he get on with it? What kind of a life is this for one of God's special children? We feel that we've learned enough, achieved enough, suffered enough, and waited enough. We're ready. So why isn't "the wonderful plan" happening?

ABANDON "MAGICAL THINKING"

Twelve years ago Michelle moved to New York, rented an apartment, and furnished it with odds and ends she had brought from home. The apartment was little more than a functional place to be when she wasn't at work. Her least favorite items in the apartment were the used dining-room furniture. The table doubled as her desk between mealtimes and was usually piled high with papers and books.

Occasionally Michelle would tell herself that since she hated the table and chairs so much, she should go out and buy a new set. But in her belief system, buying a table and chairs was something you did when you got married. To go out and buy the furniture as a single person was somehow saying that she would never get married.

A lot of single people adopt this type of "magical thinking." When I was editor of *Solo* magazine, I learned that many people wouldn't renew their subscriptions because "they didn't want to be single another year!"

In my early years of being single again, I remember thinking that I didn't ever really want to be happy as a single woman for fear that God would decide that I didn't need to be married and would cross me off of his fix-it list. I also thought if he saw how unhappy I was, he would feel sorry for me and bring a great man into my life! It's strange how God waited until I was happy as a single person before he brought a neat guy into my life on a permanent basis.

So many people keep themselves from risking, from exploring life, from experimenting and trying new things because they are waiting for someone or something to come along and make their lives special. They are afraid to do anything to rock the boat as it were, in case something worse might happen to them if they did! The key to living fully is to abandon magical thinking and to deal positively with the realities of our present lives!

CHECK YOUR PERSPECTIVE

Part of the problem we have facing reality and living fully in the present is that at times we don't understand what the plan for our lives includes. We tend to look at the present as if it were the end product. And if the end product isn't what we would consider wonderful, we want a new plan!

But we can take a lesson from David's experiences. God had reasons for sending David back to the fields. During his time in the fields, David perfected his skills on the harp and became so well known that when Saul needed soothing, he asked David to play music for him. David then became a part of the palace family as an invited guest and not as a usurper to the throne. From this position he could learn about palace life and kingly duties.

While David was in the fields, waiting, he deepened his fellowship with God. Lying under the stars and watching the beautiful sunrises and sunsets, David came to appreciate the beauty of the Creator's handiwork. David shares some of his thoughts and struggles, his discovering and rejoicing in the psalms he wrote as a shepherd in the fields.

While David spent time in the fields as a shepherd, he learned the countryside. He came to know it well—every cave, every water hole—so that when Saul tried to kill David several times and chased him through the countryside, David had the advantage and easily evaded the king.

While in the fields, David learned patience, humility, and a trust in God's timing. Once when David had an opportunity to kill Saul, he restrained himself, knowing that in God's time he would become king, but not by killing King Saul.

The time in the fields was essential to David's eventual success in achieving the exciting goals for his life.

The same is true for us. Where we are today may seem like the wrong place, and we may think that if God loved us as he says he does, he would bring on the good things a little faster. But most likely we aren't ready yet or he would! We have lessons to learn, skills to perfect, attitudes to change, areas in which we need to grow, things we need to forgive, and pasts we must leave behind.

We need to see a period of waiting as an opportunity to

prepare and get ready. Instead of feeling deserted, depressed, or disappointed, we need to ask God, "What is it that I need to learn here?"

When nothing exciting seems to be happening, do we need to develop our relational skills in order to be a better partner in that relationship God may bring us? Do we need to study managerial skills and take a class in order to be qualified for the higher-paying job the Lord may give us? Do we need to become a better steward of what the Lord has given us in order to be trusted with more?

Let's not waste time waiting. Let's spend time stretching and growing into the persons we were meant to be, into the persons we want to become.

TAKE POSITIVE ACTION

"I just got a divorce, and I got custody of myself back again!" one single woman humorously described her situation. "During my ten years of marriage, I was taken care of and told what to think. My life was planned for me. Now suddenly I'm alone and have to make all the decisions myself. It's sort of scary, but it's also exciting to be able to choose for myself!"

People who are *waiting for life to happen* don't make too many choices. And they rarely take positive action to improve their lives. Instead, they just wait, usually impatiently.

Take Charge

Take charge and wait! That may sound contradictory, but it isn't. While we rest in our trust in the Lord's will for our lives and wait for his timing to bring about the "wonderful," there are things we can do to get ready and to become better persons. We can work on our weak skills, learn lessons only experience will teach us, change negative attitudes, and as a result grow. And if we have given away control of our lives to another human being, we can redeem our lives and take charge of our selves.

Don is a good example. He has given his father the power to determine whether or not he will be happy. If his father acknowledges Don's accomplishments, Don is happy. But he's convinced that unless he receives his father's affirmation, he will never be happy again. Don needs to redefine his idea of happiness and not give his father the power to choose for him; his father may never give him the acknowledgment he wants.

Charlene thinks the only way she'll ever be fulfilled is to win the lottery so she no longer will have to work outside her home. She will stay home, care for her pets, and be happy. Until then, she will wait and hope, but not be happy. This mythical event has the power over Charlene's happiness.

Charlene and Don need to reclaim their lives. Do you? Who has control of your feelings? Who decides whether or not you will be happy, feel okay about yourself, risk new adventures, or try new skills? You do! Don't let others decide for you.

Decide what you would like someone to add to your life and add it yourself! Crystal used to say that she would like to learn to skate. She fantasized about herself and a partner skating together in perfect harmony to beautiful music. It was a wonderful dream, but the partner never came. One day she decided not to wait for a partner. She went to the skating rink and took lessons. Now she skates whenever she feels like it. Sometimes she has a partner; sometimes she skates alone. But she enjoys life now. She isn't waiting to enjoy life later.

Paul thought he shouldn't learn to cook until he owned his own home. But now rather than wait for that wonderful event to happen, he learned to cook and has a wonderful time inviting his friends over to share meals.

Wanda's fantasy was of a husband and wife playing golf together during their retirement years. Instead of waiting until then, she took lessons and plays now with friends.

Take charge of your own life. Start today.

Take Care of Yourself

Larry is like a cork floating downstream. He goes wherever the water takes him. His speed is determined by the speed of the current. His progress is slowed by debris in the water. He bounces around, to and fro, progressing only when the water around him progresses.

Larry depends on other people to make decisions for him and to take care of his needs. When he's upset, he waits for someone to notice and to ask him what's wrong. He waits for someone to notice that his car is broken down and that he needs a ride, instead of asking up-front for help. He goes with the crowd, even if it isn't his favorite type of music or play. He never suggests a place to eat but goes along with the suggestions of others. Larry stayed in a destructive dating relationship for five years, waiting for the woman to decide that she wanted out rather than making the decision himself.

Many of Larry's needs go unmet because someone has yet to notice and do something about them. That someone is going to have to be Larry. Larry must learn that as an adult in the real world, he can't wait for people to take care of him. He will have a better life when he decides to risk reaching out to make friends, to develop new skills, and to chance discomfort by making a few choices for himself.

Don't be a victim, waiting for a rescuer. What if a rescuer doesn't show up?

Become Whole

Cynthia went to a dinner for single people and sat at a table with seven men and one other woman. While the group waited for the dinner to start, Cynthia chatted with the man next to her and asked him to come over to her house for dinner the following night. He thanked her and said he couldn't come over. She pressed him, and he finally told her that he was dating someone seriously and didn't feel free to come to her house for dinner.

"Oh," she said. Then shifting gears, she leaned around him, looked at the next guy, and unabashedly asked, "Would you come to my house for dinner tomorrow night?" The guy was taken aback and didn't know what to say. In spite of her urgings, he also declined the invitation.

One by one around the table, Cynthia asked the men to have dinner with her. As each one turned her down, she became more visibly upset. When she got to the last man, she seemed desperate. With tears in her eyes, she asked him to come to her house for dinner. She offered to play the piano for him and fix whatever he wanted to eat. When the man gently explained that he would not be coming to dinner, she started to cry, "What is wrong with me? All I want is to meet some nice man, get married, and have babies!"

LEARN TO RISK

When we are that desperate to have a relationship, that hungry for love and acceptance, we end up scaring people away instead of drawing them to us. While we can admire Cynthia's persistence in trying to meet her needs, we can only feel sorry that she has not been able to find wholeness.

A friend of mine says that in order to relate well, we must not *need* to relate. If our need for a relationship is too great or too obvious, our relational skills probably need to be developed. So instead of being hungry, become whole.

A person who is emotionally insecure can't come whole into a new relationship. That person has work to do. Wholeness comes from letting go of past pain, forgiving those who have hurt us, acknowledging that people have done the best they can, and by making conscious changes in our own lives.

Become interesting. Your mother may love to hear all about how you found great bargains at Safeway, but other people may find you boring if all you can talk about is the mundane. Think about it. If you were someone else, would you date you? For how long? When was the last time you read a best-selling book, took a class, worked at a new hobby, learned a new skill, or had an adventure? Instead of being someone who wants to meet people, become the type of person other people want to meet!

Get involved with life! I once went to a seminar at which people were trying to stretch their comfort zones. One woman admitted she was deathly afraid of being in front of large groups. So, of course, her assignment was just that: to do an exercise routine in front of all of us. She was panic stricken. I've never seen a person so afraid. For hours before it was her turn, she paced, trembled, wrung her hands, and chewed her fingernails. She was a wreck.

When she went to the front of the group, she was so pathetic that each of us in the audience felt sorry for her. We shared in her agony. We resented the leaders for being so cruel. The assignment was obviously too much for her. The music started, and she made a few halting movements. Except for the music, the room was silent. We could hear her short, hard breathing. The tension mounted as the seconds ticked by.

After a few minutes, which seemed like hours, the leaders signaled to a man to come forward and join the woman. The man, obviously at ease, gave her a friendly smile and began doing the exercises with her. What a difference! Suddenly she relaxed, forgot we were there, and followed his lead. They wound up the routine and finished with a flourish and exaggerated bows. We applauded.

Next the leaders put on a fast record and told us to join in the exercising. The mood changed. We twisted, turned, touched our toes, kicked our legs, and jogged in place. Some of us were not used to such exercise, but nobody cared. We were having fun. After about ten minutes, the music stopped and we sat down.

One of the leaders told us to look around the room and notice the look on everyone's faces. What I saw were rosy cheeks, sparkling eyes, smiles, relaxed shoulders, and an aliveness I'll never forget. The leader told us to memorize that look. He chided us gently. "You should have seen yourselves a few minutes ago. White cheeks, pinched eyebrows, pained faces, frowns. All of you were upset and sharing in the woman's fears. That's what observers look like. People who don't participate but go through life observing and judging. But the look you have now is the look of people who are involved with life, and it's not a look you can fake. Watch for it. And when you find it, you'll find people who are alive and involved in life, people who are attractive. It will show in their faces."

I've found that statement to be true. When I speak to a crowd of people, I can tell which are observers of life and which are *actively involved in living life!*

Get involved. Become attractive! Become whole!

MAKE FRIENDS WITH GOD

I know a woman who is a personal friend of a world-famous singer. Several times a year she goes to his shows, meets him backstage, drives home in his limousine, and has a late dinner and a midnight swim with his band and other friends. For days after she comes back, she is the center of attention at the office as her coworkers want to hear all of the details and participate vicariously in her friendship. Our friendships make us interesting people.

Who better to become friends with than God himself? God is more than the Creator, more than the Savior, and more than a rescuer to turn to in times of trouble. He is our friend.

When we are friends with someone, we tend to become like that person in many ways. As we become closer friends with God, we will be more open to becoming the persons he designed us to be, to become more like him.[7]

Jesus tells us that we are his friends if we follow his commands. His greatest command is to love each other the way he loves us.[8]

One of the ways he shows his love for us is his constant presence with us through the Holy Spirit. The Gospels refer to the Holy Spirit as the comforter, the one who "comes alongside us" as we face the difficulties and joys of life.[9] Isn't that an apt description of a true friend? One who comforts, who comes alongside us.

Come Alongside

Dave was a recreational runner. He didn't go in for the marathons. He just enjoyed getting out in the early mornings and running a few miles every day. One day he and his friend Nate decided to condition themselves for a fifteen-kilometer race. Dave developed a plan for the big day. He would set himself a comfortable pace for the first half of the race and then would pour on the energy for the last seven and a half kilometers.

The day of the race was beautiful. Everything was going according to plan as the race started. Dave found a good steady pace and was running well. The kilometers ticked by. Just as he saw the halfway marker and started to push, the road turned and went straight uphill. Surprised, Dave began to talk out loud. "I can't make that hill!" he panted. "I think I'd better drop out now!"

But Nate had come up behind him in time to hear his comments and urged him not to stop. "Come on, Dave," Nate urged, "you can do it. I'll pace it with you." He matched his steps to Dave's, and step by step they began to run together. Gathering new energy from the encouragement, Dave headed up the hill. Step by step, Dave and Nate finished the race together.

Nate probably would have had less success if he had yelled, "Come on, Dave, follow me. I'll show you how to do it!" or if he had dropped out of the race to cheer Dave along by applauding. Nate might have gotten Dave to finish the race if he had offered to run behind him and step on his heels! But none of those ways would have given Dave as much energy and courage to continue as Nate's running with him did. There's power in coming alongside to help.

Zig Ziglar tells the story of a little girl who lived in a basement cell of a state institution.[10] Although most of the staff treated the girl as if she were incorrigible, one nurse thought she saw something in little Annie's eyes. She decided to sit outside the girl's cell to eat her lunch everyday.

For weeks the girl made no response to the nurse's presence. One day the nurse left a brownie for the little girl, and when she returned later, the brownie was gone. After months of just being there, eating her lunch beside the girl, the nurse began to see a change in little Annie, and she knew she had made contact. The changes continued, and soon afterward Annie was moved upstairs to live with the more well-behaved residents. Annie made remarkable progress and later left the institution, saying she wanted to someday work with the handicapped. All because a nurse cared enough to come alongside a little girl long enough to make a difference in her life.

Little Annie realized her ambition. And when Helen Keller received one of England's highest honors, she said she owed it all to her teacher, Anne Sullivan, who had been little Annie in a state institution many years before. The world owes a lot to Helen Keller for sharing with us the miracle of her incredible experiences. Helen Keller owes a lot to Anne Sullivan, who came alongside her. And Anne Sullivan owes a lot to a nurse, who owes a lot to who knows whom.

I will always be grateful to the many people who came alongside me during the hard times in my life. I pray that I have been faithful in coming alongside others who have needed the encouragement and strength of having someone pace it with them.

GO THE DISTANCE

"Seriously," Annette shares with a friend, "I try not to focus on waiting for the knight in shining armor or the big job or the dream opportunity. I try to grow and to improve myself. But I wonder how long I'm supposed to wander around getting better and better! When will God do something special in my life?"

I know that feeling! Sometimes the waiting can seem so fruitless. However, I have come to believe that God's wonderful plan for our lives is not just whatever good and terrific surprises he plans to give us. His wonderful plan for us, like his plan for David, also includes the struggles, the time spent out tending the sheep, learning the tedious lessons of life, and the quiet times when we are just alone with God. He does have a wonderful plan for our lives; the plan includes whatever is happening to us *now*.

When I get weary from "tending sheep," I must remind myself that God promises to give me the strength to hang in there. He promises to give me the strength to fly upward like an eagle, to run without getting tired, to walk without fainting.[11] It seems to me that I usually have the energy for the big difficulties, the crises, the major problems. The old adrenaline pumps in, and I find strength. But it is the walking, the day-by-day, unexciting march that gets to me. I need the strength to walk and not faint in order to go the distance.

If your life seems tiring, and like David, nothing special seems to be happening, don't give up. Look to God for strength and trust his promises. And don't "get tired of doing what is right, for after a while [you] will reap a harvest of blessing if [you] don't get discouraged and give up."[12] Go the distance!

✓ SELF-ASSESSMENT AND FOLLOW-UP

1. Are you in a "waiting" or an "action" mode? Check those statements that best describe you.

DON'T WAIT FOR THE "WONDERFUL"

Waiting

___ When I make a new friend, I wait for him or her to make the first call to reconnect.

___ I have several vacation dreams I'm waiting to try out when I find a friend to go with me.

___ I've always thought I'd like to go back to school someday.

___ I often think that one day I'd like to try a different lifestyle, career, hairstyle, or car, but I haven't yet.

___ Basically, I'm a procrastinator.

___ When things go wrong, I usually sit tight and hope they'll get better.

Action

___ If I like someone, I initiate contact.

___ I plan and take creative vacations each year.

___ I take a college class nearly every semester.

___ I'm forever trying new things and activities.

___ When I think of something that needs doing, I usually spring into action and get it done.

___ When I have a problem, I go to work on solving it.

Are you more of a waiter than a doer? Set some goals this week to begin changing that area of your life.

2. Consider what things you are waiting for in your life. What can you do to make these things happen? Are they really worth waiting for? Are they actually going to occur?

3. Make this week "Something New Week."
Eat a new food.
Try a new sport.
Read a new book.
Make a new friend.
Buy a new article of clothing.
Use a new word and make it part of your working vocabulary.
Listen to a new kind of music.
Try a new radio station.

Try a new hairstyle.
Wear a "new" color.
Learn about something new.

After the week is over, write in your journal about how focusing on the "new and different" influenced your attitude.

4. Make a list of things you need to do around the house. Try to do eighty percent of the list this week. Reflect on how it feels to clear up most of the list.

5. Reach out to someone who is shut in because of illness, age, or handicap. Find ways to bring a note of kindness and cheer to that person.

✒ GROUP INTERACTION

1. **Discussion.** Use the following discussion starters to get everyone involved. Work in groups of 5–10, giving each person a chance to complete the first statement before the group moves on to the next one. If a person is uncomfortable sharing, that person may pass.

   a. Sometimes I feel God has put me on the back burner because. . . .

   b. I can identify with David in that. . . .

   c. What I think I'm supposed to be learning right now is. . . .

   d. What I really hope that God will do in my life in the next few months is. . . .

   e. One way I've grown in the last six months is. . . .

   f. If I took seriously what this chapter says, I would have to. . . .

   g. One way I'm going to change my life in this next week is. . . .

   h. My prayer life lately seems to be. . . .

   i. A neat answer to prayer I've received recently was. . . .

   j. I could use support from this group in the area of. . . .

2. **Stories.** Work in groups of two to three to write a modern parable about a person who lives his or her life waiting for *life* to happen. Share your stories.

3. **Posters.** Draw colorful posters illustrating one of the main points of this chapter. Share your posters. Exchange them and take them home to hang up for a week as reminders.

4. **Group Singing.** Look through hymnbooks or chorus books and find three songs that reflect the ideas in this chapter. Sing them together.

7
Learn to Be Open, Honest, and Caring

One of my favorite things to do in a seminar on building relationships is to have the group come up with a list of characteristics they would like to find in a dating partner. One of the lists looked like this:

kind	gentle
affectionate	sensitive
rich	sense of humor
can be confronted	can share feelings
understanding	conscientious
no phoney masks	reliable
likes to work	active in church
likes kids	loving
athletic	sociable
loves me	handles money well
caring	trustworthy
open	can confront well
practicing Christian	good listener
faithful	honest
loves God	friendly
shares easily	

With few exceptions, the characteristics can be loosely grouped under three categories: openness, honesty, and caring. The seminar participants discuss the fact that our most basic human need is to be loved and accepted. And in the process of trying to fill that need, we seek people who are open, honest, and caring.

LEARN TO BE OPEN, HONEST, AND CARING

Then we examine the question: "If we are all looking for openness, honesty, and caring, why haven't we found what we are looking for in each other?" As we talk, we discover several reasons.

PRINCIPLES OF SOWING AND REAPING

Loving, caring relationships are some of the most special gifts God has given us. We all need love and attention from others. It feels so good to have another person tell us we are special, that they enjoy spending time with us, that we are fun, or that we have been helpful to them in their journey through life.

Yet all too often, we don't actually hear those words from others. Instead, we are left to conclude that people like spending time with us because they do it or that they enjoy our company because they seem to be having a good time when we are together. But why don't we say the words?

One reason we don't say the affirming words to each other is because we haven't yet grasped the principles of sowing and reaping. The Bible tells us that we reap what we sow.[1] We find this principle to be true in all areas of nature and life. Lecturer Jim Rohn talks of seven simple but powerful principles of the sowing and reaping process.[2] Let's examine these principles as they apply to relationships.

You Must Sow to Reap

Imagine a farmer who has only one cup of corn and who doesn't want to risk it on bad soil. He goes around to different parcels of land and says, "Show me the type of corn you can raise, and then I'll decide whether or not to invest my one cup of corn in you." Ridiculous! You can't get any credit from the ground; before you can reap, you have to invest. You have to take a chance. You have to make the first move.

And the same holds true in relationships. Before you can reap openness, you must be open. Before you will find honesty and caring in relationships, you must demonstrate those characteristics yourself.

Diane hasn't learned the value of sowing before you reap. "When I have a close, romantic relationship, I plan to learn how to confront lovingly without bursting into tears and freezing up," she explains. But if Diane doesn't learn to confront lovingly *before* she has a relationship, her plan probably won't work.

Jonathan has a similar problem. Most people see Jonathan as cold, closed, and somewhat mechanical because he doesn't express emotion visibly or verbally. Jonathan wants to be more open and hopes someday to find a relationship in which he will feel secure enough to express his emotions freely.

Both Diane and Jonathan are afraid to risk investing themselves in any relationship that is less than the perfect one. And so far neither of them has found that perfect relationship. However, if they should decide to go ahead and become the open and honest people they plan to become, they might find close friends among the people they already know. Or maybe they would even find the romantic partners they seek.

Sometimes we don't find open, honest, and caring relationships because we are afraid to risk. We've been hurt, and we don't want to be rejected again. Sometimes we aren't ready to have that level of interaction. Sometimes we just don't know how to sow the qualities we want to find. We've never developed the skills or had the experience of having a great relationship.

Whatever the reason, we have to take the risk and make the first move. We must sow before we can reap.

You Reap What You Sow

What would you think of a farmer who was out in a wheat field, throwing a temper tantrum because he had wanted corn to grow there even though he had planted wheat? The guy should be locked up, right? Everyone knows that you reap what you sow. If you want green beans, you sow green beans, not tomatoes.

So why do we sometimes go looking for a crop we don't plant? Why do we expect people to reach out to us when we haven't reached out to them? Why do we think people should be kind and caring when we haven't been kind and caring first?

I was once in a seminar where small groups were told to examine relationships. Having already been at the seminar for

LEARN TO BE OPEN, HONEST, AND CARING

eight hours, I was tired. I took one look at the other three people in my group and my heart sank. Trying not to let my thoughts show on my face, I thought, *Of all the people in this room, why did they have to put me with these three? I don't see anything here I like!* But, trying to be the good participant, I entered into the assignment.

The first question was "How are you in a relationship?" When it was my turn to answer, I tried to give an accurate picture of myself. "I'm a good friend. I'm open about my feelings and take responsibility for my needs. I'm learning to confront in a gentle and caring way...." Halfway through my answer one of the other members of my group stopped me.

"Are you really an open and caring person?" he challenged. "I don't see that. You aren't being open with us. You don't really seem to want to be here."

I tried to explain that I was open after I got to know people. And that most of my friends would say I was a very caring person.

"We might become your friends," he continued gently, "if you gave us a chance. You are being very closed. We can't get in!"

And he was right. I hadn't realized before that the qualities I liked in myself as a friend didn't extend to people I didn't know. I had some changes to make in my life if I was going to be a genuinely open, honest, and caring person.

If we sow from bitterness, anger, fear, or a critical spirit, we will tend to reap the same from others. But if we sow kindness, acceptance, and encouragement, we will be given those in return. "If you give, you will get! Your gift will return to you in full and overflowing measure, pressed down, shaken together to make room for more, and running over. Whatever measure you use to give—large or small—will be used to measure what is given back to you."[3]

Alex is one of those warm people everyone loves to know. He seems to like everyone and makes even new acquaintances feel special as he includes them in his activities. He never hesitates to introduce himself or take the first risk in a new relationship. People respond in kind. Everyone wants to be in Alex's circle of friends.

You Reap More Than You Sow

How much farming do you suppose would be done if a farmer started with one cup of corn, planted it, did all of the work to get it to grow and be healthy, invested three months of his life into the crop, and all he ended up with was one cup of corn? Not much. But the payoff in sowing and reaping is that you reap much more than you sow. For each cup of corn you sow, you may reap as much as a bushel!

In life the same is true. You reap much more than you sow. If you are kind, you will reap kindness from those around you. If you are a loving person, other people will love you back. But if you are bitter, resentful, angry, or critical, most of your world will be angry and critical toward you. And the return on the investment can be overwhelming.

Fran is a very thoughtful person. She sends cards just to say hi. She is always ready to give a warm hug or go out for coffee and encouragement. She has a way of stopping whatever she is doing to give you her full attention when you drop by her desk or her house. And everyone loves Fran, not for what she does, but for who she is. She sows from a spirit of caring and concern.

Sheila, on the other hand, sows just the opposite. She seems to be perpetually scowling. She is usually so distracted and behind in her work that if you try to talk with her, you get only a fragment of her attention. She is a chronic complainer and always is ready with a caustic remark about a coworker. Underneath her outward appearance and behaviors, Sheila may be a very nice person, but few people take the time to find out. Most people leave her alone and don't treat her with kindness and concern. You reap more than what you sow!

You Must Be Patient

Let's say that the farmer has planted his corn. Does he come back the next day with a bushel basket to harvest the crop? Does he give it a couple more days, then come back again ready to either harvest the crop or dig up the seed and plant it elsewhere? No! Raising crops takes time, work, and patience.

Tim has yet to find the woman of his dreams. He has his system figured out. He allows a woman four dates. If after that

LEARN TO BE OPEN, HONEST, AND CARING

she hasn't proven to him that she would be the perfect wife (and believe me, he has a long list she would have to fulfill), then he breaks off the relationship and moves on to another woman. He has just about run out of women to date.

Beth allows herself one fight with a dating partner. If he can't handle the argument in a manner she feels would be productive in a long-term relationship, then the dating is over.

Dexter likes to take a woman out to coffee for a first date and just talk. He judges the potential for a relationship based on whether or not they are able to get to a feeling level of conversation during the first few minutes. If not, he eliminates her from his list of potential intimate friends.

Edward, on the other hand, has learned that relationships take time to develop. When there is a minor problem with a new friendship, he chalks it up to individual differences and doesn't make a big deal of it. He acknowledges the difference of opinion, perception, taste, or preferred behavior and continues to explore the friendship. He has several good friends now he might have missed if he had let a few initial differences become unacceptable.

Relationships take time, work, and patience to develop. If we don't take the time to develop friendships, we may end up without any friends, just as the farmer would be without a crop if he tried to harvest it before the seeds had time to develop.

Sometimes You Lose

We've all heard stories of farmers who do everything right and yet end up losing their crop. They prepared the soil, planted the seed, built the scarecrows, watched over the crop, watered, weeded, and cared for the plants. Then the day before the harvest, an unexpected hailstorm or tornado wipes out the crop. The farmer didn't do anything wrong, but he lost.

In relationships, sometimes we lose. Harry's best friend got a promotion and moved six states away. Harry misses him more than he can express. Jeremy's wife died in a car accident. Theirs had been a "perfect" marriage. He can't believe she is gone. Beverly had given her best effort to making her dating relationship work. She didn't do anything wrong, but Scott wasn't ready to get married and settle down, so he drifted away. Mary and Nancy used to spend every Saturday afternoon quilting. After four years, Nancy decided she had had enough of quilting and took up tennis. Mary had no interest in tennis and wanted to continue quilting. Their friendship continued, but on a different level because they no longer spent hours talking over the quilts they were making.

Sometimes you lose. People move on, move out, or move away. And when there is a loss, our lives change in response.

When You Lose, You Must Plant Again

When the farmer loses everything to the tornado, he not only doesn't have a harvest but he also loses his initial cup of corn. What can he do? He could give up. He could say, "That's it. I gave it my best shot. I held back nothing. I really worked at this and look what happened! Never again will I let a crop make a fool out of me! From now on, I will be in my living room, watching television. If a crop wants to find me, it can just march into my living room!" Or he can acknowledge his losses, draw on his resources, borrow some corn, and plant again next year. It's obvious which option has the better chance of yielding a crop the next year.

Too many single people, after being hurt or rejected in a relationship, just give up and refuse to risk ever reaching out again. Jack is a good example. When he got cancer, his wife left him because she couldn't stand being around sick people. Today, even though he is in remission and his prognosis is very good, Jack won't even talk to a woman alone, and dating is out of the question.

Vera dates a lot but never lets a relationship get serious because she doesn't want to be hurt again the way she was when her husband divorced her after twenty years of marriage.

Guy did poorly on a promotional interview examination, so now he refuses to compete for any openings, even when encouraged to do so by his boss.

George tried to learn to water ski. He couldn't get up out of the water on the skis the first couple of times he tried, so he gave up. He simply won't try again.

Wilma had been dumped by a second boyfriend and was tempted to give up on relationships with all men. But after a time of healing from the rejection, she risked trusting again.

Now Wilma is happily married and glad she was willing to take a risk.

When you lose, you must try again.

If You Don't Like the Crop, Talk to the Sower

This is perhaps the most important of the principles. We are responsible for the "crops" in our lives. We are the sowers. We decide what goes into our lives. If we don't like what is going on, then we need to tell ourselves to change what we are planting!

Harry spent every lunch hour loudly complaining about his peanut-butter-and-jelly sandwiches. Finally one of his coworkers leaned over and said, "Harry, if you don't like peanut butter and jelly, why don't you ask your wife to put something else into your lunch?"

"You leave my wife out of this," Harry retorted instantly. "I pack my own lunch!"

Often we are like Harry. We complain about the lack of friendships, love, laughter, or joy in our lives. We hate where we work, where we live, and what we do for fun. But we "pack" our own lives! If we don't have enough friends, we can make some. If we don't like where we live, we can move! If we hate our jobs, we can learn new skills and look for new jobs!

If we don't like the crop, we may need to sit down and have a long talk with the sower—ourselves.

SEASONS OF SOWING AND REAPING

There are seasons or phases in the sowing and reaping process in life, just as there are in farming. There is a time to plan, invest, learn, build, cultivate, and work. Only afterward do we have the joy of the reward. But there are winter times when nothing seems to grow and when we get no return on our investment.

Linda hasn't had a date for months. Even though she goes to church and stays around for coffee and conversation afterward, nothing seems to happen. Even though she is friendly and outgoing, no one seems to be interested.

Barry is an artist. He hasn't been able to come up with a

new song for almost six months, and he's beginning to wonder if he's lost his ability to write songs.

Linda and Barry are living in a winter mode. Winters can be hard times, times when we are struggling just to survive, let alone grow. During the winters of life, I rely on biblical promises such as "Your strength will equal your days."[4] Although winters may seem cold and hard, they also can be times to reflect, study, recuperate, regroup, heal, or renew.

But after the winter comes the spring. Every year, like clockwork. You can count on it. Spring brings new energy, new hope, and new opportunities. After Barry's winter of not being able to write, he bounced into spring; he wrote an entire album in just two months.

At the end of one of the winters of my life, I read a magazine story that seemed to be about a character who had feelings similar to mine. Scattered words and phrases seemed to leap from the page to form a poem of feelings I shared with the storyteller.

RETURN TO LIFE

The winter world
Mirrors my soul,
A pattern of warm colors
Now drained
   To dull browns.

And, yet, I'm caught in a
   Fantasy,
     Freefalling
       Through the frightening
Gap of your
Absence.

Yet without my fantasy
Tomorrow
Would seem
But another chore,
   Unrelieved,
     Unwanted,
       Unwelcome.

LEARN TO BE OPEN, HONEST, AND CARING

Some days reality intervenes
As the fantasy is seared off by
  Raw anger,
    Unbearable pain,
      Or another loss.

Still I resurrect the dream,
And hope renews.
The raw edges of pain,
  Buffed smooth
    and numbed.
Once again I am sure
  I can cope.

Coping.
Making the
  Appropriate moves
  And gestures,
Empty actions
  Not real.
Coping is waiting
  For life.

Soon the fantasy will fade,
No longer needed,
When despite
  The cold fear
  Inside my soul,
I leap
  From the edge
    Of hurt
Back into the
  Rough
    and
      Tumble
Center of life!

    Spring is a time to tell yourself to get out of the house and back out into the community, the singles' group, the job market, and the dating scene. It's when you decide to try again, this time with hope. Spring is a time of renewed energy, when we know that we must get to work and do what needs to be done now.[5]

After the planting comes the summertime, when the warm sunshine can make us lazy. Pulling weeds isn't exactly how we would like to spend our afternoons. Summer is a time of relaxing and enjoying the respite from our labors. It's vacation time. In life, I think the summertimes are when we are drifting along, things are going okay, and we don't feel the urgency to keep pushing or to be attentive to our sowing.

But summer is also a time to watch that we don't let people fall through the cracks in our lives. We need to be vigilant, for if we aren't careful, we can procrastinate and lose our momentum.[6]

The fall seasons of life are probably the most exciting and the most revealing because that's when we reap from our investments. Fall is exciting if we have sown good seeds and cared for our crops well. It's revealing because we can see if we have indeed sown what we wanted to reap.

It's hard for me to watch some of my friends make choices I'm sure are unwise, because I know that soon will come the "fall," when they reap the consequences of their choices. No matter how many times I tried to reason with one friend, Mike, about how important attendance was on the job, he refused to be on the job every day, on time. I never did understand how he could have been shocked when he was terminated for poor attendance. And yet I felt so sorry for his having lost such a good job.

I shouldn't be too surprised, though. We all learn by doing. If telling worked, we would all be perfect because we have all been *told* how to behave—from parents, teachers, pastors, friends, and countless other people.

After the harvests in our lives, we should stop and take stock. Just how did we get where we are and end up with what we did? What changes would we like to make next time? What could we do differently or better? And what things do we want to continue?

As we grow in our relationships, we can take steps to become more open, honest, and caring.

LEARN TO BE OPEN, HONEST, AND CARING

MOVE TOWARD OPENNESS

Andrea has a problem being open because people have betrayed her by telling other people things she had said in confidence. Andrea was also raised in a very judgmental home, so she frequently feels criticized when people differ with her ideas or viewpoints. This has caused her to be fairly quiet around people until she comes to know them well enough to predict their responses to her.

Ross has been learning to risk increased openness. When he is planning to share something he's not quite comfortable with, he prefaces it with verbal warning signs like these: "I'm a little hesitant about sharing this, but...." or "I'm not sure you're going to agree with this, but I think...." or "I may be wrong, but I think...."

This technique can be helpful at first when learning to share something potentially controversial. However, as Ross becomes more comfortable with being open, he will be able to share his opinions without these verbal crutches.

You can become more open in relationships by practicing self-disclosure, by listening to feedback from others, and by being more trusting in relationships. Here are some ideas for practicing openness:

- Ask several people to rate your openness. If they feel you're an open person, ask them to tell you what makes them feel that way. If they feel you're not open, ask them to explain.
- In your journal, write down two lists: one of the significant people in your life; one of several topics of conversation, ranging from very personal to general. Then note which types of communication you have with the different people in your life. With whom are you most open? With whom are you most guarded? Why? Practice being more open with two people this week. See what happens.
- Think about your friends. How open are they? Why do you suppose you chose these people as friends? Spend more time this week with your more open friends. Does this make a difference in how open you are?
- For this month, set and work on four goals that will

increase your openness. Write the goals in your journal and evaluate your progress at the end of the month.
- In your journal, write five affirmations about being open (e.g., "I'm free to share my feelings."). Then find a Scripture verse that supports being open. Practice saying these affirmations to yourself several times a day.
- Keep a journal log of each new type of self-disclosure you practice during the next week. At the end of the week, evaluate how it felt to be open.

MOVE TOWARD HONESTY

"Do you really mean that genuine Christians can be dishonest in relationships?" Debbie asked at a recent seminar.

Yes, Debbie, most people are somewhat less than honest in their relationships. Not that dishonesty is always outright lying. Dishonesty can take several forms.

Toni frequently agrees to baby-sit for friends because she's afraid to hurt their feelings by saying no. Toni hates to baby-sit, but a lot of people don't know that. So she gets frequent requests. All during the evening with the children, Toni is resentful because she feels her friends are taking advantage of her. Toni isn't honest in that area of her relationships.

It's okay to do something you don't enjoy, as long as the choice is yours and you don't turn around and resent your friends in the process. But you can learn to be honest by recognizing your limitations and living within them. You can learn to recognize your right to have preferences and ideas and learn to say no when appropriate.

Vern was honest when his father-in-law, Bill, offered to pay for a trip to Paris for both couples, plus Bill's mother and son. Vern thanked his father-in-law but said he didn't like taking group vacations. At first Bill was hurt because his gift had been rejected. Then after considering the situation, Bill thanked Vern for being honest enough to admit what he did and didn't want. Bill gave his daughter and Vern the trip anyway (and Bill and the others went at a different time). Afterward the two couples grew closer because they were able

LEARN TO BE OPEN, HONEST, AND CARING

to share about similar experiences in Paris. Vern and his wife had enjoyed their trip, as had Bill and his wife. How different the outcome would have been if Vern had been afraid to say no and had gone along on the group vacation. All of the time they were together, Vern might have been resentful and unhappy. The trip memories would have been painful, not something to enjoy later.

If you need to develop honesty in your relationships, try these exercises.

- Spend a whole day being aware of several different interactions in your life. Write them down in your journal and compare your honesty in the situations, your thought responses to each one, and your feelings about what happened.
- List several typical interactions you experience. Which ones make you feel good? Sad? Angry? Hurt? Puzzled? Why is your response different in different situations?
- Practice asking clarifying questions in conversations, for example: What did you mean by that? How could we do this better? What are your ideas about this?
- Read one or two books about honesty in communications, for example: *The Secret of Staying in Love* by John Powell and *Caring Enough to Confront* by David Augsburger. List in your journal five things to begin practicing in your own relationships.
- Roleplay an interaction you want to have with someone. Practice your responses so that you will feel more comfortable doing it.
- Try writing a contract in a close relationship. Agree to help each other in one particular area.
- Study biblical interactions and commitments. Note the characters' experiences and compare them with your own.
- Write five affirmations about being more honest. Find Scripture verses to support these affirmations; then practice the affirmations several times each day.

MOVE TOWARD CARING

"I think it's easier to be open and honest than it is to be caring in a male-female relationship, at least in the beginning," Joanne shares. "Who wants to be the one to say 'I love you' first and have the other person simply say, 'That's nice!'?"

A lot of people may agree with Joanne. It's hard to determine just how friendly one can be to a member of the opposite sex before the other person gets the message that we care about him or her in a special way. I've known people who have a strong tendency to fall deeply "in love" almost instantly. By the end of the first date, they are thinking marriage. After a couple of dates, they want to send out joint holiday cards. This creates a problem when only one partner in the relationship feels this deeply. Single people with such tendencies need to develop smaller steps to love and allow their partners time to reciprocate. It is desirable to love people but we need to be cautious when being "in love" so we don't rush into premature relationships.

You can express Christian love, agape love, in relationships by initiating contact, expressing positive emotions, investing time together, and showing love and affection. If you have problems expressing this kind of love in relationships, try these practical ideas:

- Tell a friend how you really feel about him or her, emphasizing the loving aspects of your relationship.
- Write a letter to someone you admire and let that person know just how much you like and respect him or her.
- Spend an evening expressing your love for a friend or dating partner. Be the giver all evening. Tell the person things you appreciate about him or her. Show that you care by serving the person's favorite refreshments.
- Practice saying "I love you" to your parents, friends, dating partner, and children, particularly if you aren't used to saying it.
- Buy a sentimental card and send it to a friend, expressing your love and friendship.
- Write a poem about how much you enjoy a friend and share the poem with that person.

LEARN TO BE OPEN, HONEST, AND CARING

- Write five affirmations about being a caring, loving person. Find Scripture verses to support these affirmations. Practice saying them several times a day.

SOWING SEEDS

Open, honest, and caring. How would you rate yourself in relationships? Do you have a lot of good relationships? You may want to look at the principles of sowing and reaping and how they apply to your life.

Jesus told a story of a farmer who went out to sow seeds in his field.[7] He had good seed and a plan. He was going to sow plentifully. And he did.

Some of the seed fell on the hard path, and the birds swooped down and ate it. The birds got the seed! Some people are like that type of soil. They hear a lot of great ideas at the different singles' conferences, seminars, and meetings they attend, but the ideas just seem to fly right out the window. The birds get the seeds! These people are observers of life. They say, "Ho-hum, just another speech." They have a lot of excuses for things not going right in their lives. If you offered them a gold mine, these people might be like the miner's neighbor who said he couldn't dig in the rich mine because he didn't have a shovel, and new ones cost a whole lot! Observers play it safe. Their harvest is poor.

Some of the seeds fell on shallow, rocky soil, where the sun soon withered the young plants. Some people are like this rocky soil. They are gung-ho starters. They say, "Let's do it!" They get up early the next morning after a seminar and start three life changes before nine o'clock. They are ready! But when the going gets tough and the heat is on, they falter and wither on the vine. They are always ready to go, but they never go the distance.

Some seed fell on thorny soil, where the weeds and thorns choked the life out of the plant. We all know people like this. They have good intentions, but they always find a few thorns in the way of getting the job done. They have to finish other things first. Their priorities aren't in the right order, and they procrastinate. "Sounds great," they say. "Someday I must do something about that." But they rarely do.

LEARN TO RISK

Some seed fell on good soil and grew to full maturity. Thank goodness we also have some people in the world who are like fertile soil. They say, "I'm going to turn my life around," and they do. Some get a hundred percent return, some sixty percent, and some thirty percent. But they all grow.

What soil are you most like?

✔ SELF-ASSESSMENT AND FOLLOW-UP

1. Think of a person with whom you have a close relationship. Check the sentences that describe you in that relationship.

   ___ I'm not afraid to share my feelings.

   ___ I can disagree without getting into an argument.

   ___ I can raise controversial subjects and discuss them freely.

   ___ I can receive negative feedback without being devastated.

   ___ My friends can count on my honesty.

   ___ I give my friends the benefit of the doubt and don't start accusing them right away.

   ___ I treat my friends the way I want to be treated.

   ___ I freely express my affection.

   ___ We do things that we both really enjoy.

   ___ I show my affection by doing things for my friends.

   Do you feel you are open, honest, and caring in this relationship? Count the number of sentences you checked and multiply it by ten to get a percentage of your openness, honesty, and caring in these issues.

2. Set a goal to implement three to five of this chapter's suggestions for being open, honest, and caring. Write the goals in your journal and check your progress after a week.

LEARN TO BE OPEN, HONEST, AND CARING

✓ GROUP INTERACTION

1. **Discussion.** Use the following discussion starters to get everyone involved. Work in groups of 5–10, giving each person a chance to complete the first statement before the group moves on to the next one. If a person is uncomfortable sharing, that person may pass.

   Openness. Read 1 Timothy 4:12 and use the verse as the basis for completing some of the following statements:

   a. The person I'm very open with is. . . .
   b. The person I'm least open with is. . . .
   c. If I were open with that person, I think that. . . .
   d. What keeps me from being more open is. . . .
   e. Mostly I'm afraid that. . . .
   f. I'd like to be more open about. . . .
   g. I once risked openness, and it was a disaster because. . . .
   h. I once risked openness, and it worked out well because. . . .
   i. This week I could be more open by. . . .
   j. What the above verse says to me about openness is. . . .

   Honesty. Read Hebrews 4:12–13 and use the passage as the basis for completing some of the following statements:

   a. Honesty is hard for me when. . . .
   b. The problem with being honest with people is that. . . .
   c. The people who are most honest with me are. . . .
   d. When someone is less than honest with me, I feel. . . .
   e. Ways I make it hard for people to be honest with me are. . . .
   f. Ways I make it easy for people to be honest with me are. . . .
   g. I once risked honesty, and it was difficult because. . . .
   h. I feel that hiding strong emotions is dishonest because. . . .
   i. One way I could be more honest this week is. . . .

j. What the above Scripture passage says to me about honesty is. . . .

Caring. Read John 13:35 and use this verse as the basis for completing some of the following statements:

a. To me caring means. . . .

b. I find it fairly easy to care when. . . .

c. It's almost impossible for me to risk caring when. . . .

d. I once risked caring, and it was a disaster because. . . .

e. I once risked caring, and it worked well because. . . .

f. I've learned that I need to prepare myself for caring by. . . .

g. A caring gesture I've been considering for a while is. . . .

h. If I risked caring more, my life would be. . . .

i. A caring risk I plan to take this week is. . . .

j. What the above Scripture passage says to me about caring is. . . .

2. **List.** Compile a list of barriers to being open, honest, and caring. Rank the barriers in order of difficulty, with 1 representing the most difficult to overcome. Discuss ways to eliminate the barriers.

3. **Roleplay.** On separate sheets of paper, write out several situations involving openness, honesty, and caring. Then have two people at a time go to the front of the group, draw a paper, and roleplay the situation. Discuss why it's hard or easy in real life to be open, honest, or caring in that situation.

4. **Panel Discussion.** Divide into three work teams. One team should prepare a five-minute presentation focusing on openness, one team on honesty, and one team on caring. Elect one person from each group to make the presentation and represent the group's point of view on the panel. Discuss the points made by each panel member.

8
Risk Reaching Out

For years I was shy in social settings when it came to one-on-one conversation with men. I rarely initiated conversation, convinced that they would think I was stupid, boring, or foolish! Self-doubts plagued me, eroding my self-confidence.

However, I remember one social function when I had none of those doubts. I had been watching a thrilling World Series ball game all afternoon. Turning to a man seated nearby, I commented excitedly, "Wasn't that a spectacular catch Reggie Jackson made this afternoon?" At that time the only sports interest I had was to watch the World Series each year. So it wasn't often that I could confidently initiate a conversation about sports. It felt good! For a moment.

The man looked at me blankly. "I'm not into sports," he said, before turning away again to stare quietly at all the other people mingling, talking, and laughing.

Reaching out is risky! Sometimes it doesn't work. Sometimes we lose. Sometimes we feel foolish. But the key is the word *sometimes*; because sometimes it *does* work. Sometimes we win. And sometimes reaching out makes us feel great! It's these positive results that make the risk worth taking.

But all too often, we don't take the risk. We don't take the initiative with other people. Why is that? A lot of single people ask me about meeting and making friends of the opposite sex. I hear comments such as: "I can't find any men (women)" or "I can't make contact" or "I can't get a date!"

WHAT'S THE PROBLEM?

Let's look at why we find it hard to make contact with other people.

Finding People Is Not the Problem

Finding people to reach out to isn't difficult at all. We talk to people all the time. We ask store clerks (or other shoppers) for the location of desired items. We ask directions. We comment on the weather. We ask the time. If something unusual occurs, we turn to anyone nearby and ask, "Did you see that?"

People are everywhere: at work, the store, post office, gas station, church, parties, concerts, in the next apartment, house, or block.

We can find people everywhere! Lots of them. And according to national statistics, about half of those people are single!

Meeting People Is Not the Problem

Initiating casual contact is not very difficult. A friend of mine moved into a new area and threw a party. He distributed flyers stating that he was new and wanted to get to know his neighbors. Over forty-five people showed up.

Susie offered her home for a potluck to the Sunday-school class at church. She met lots of new people. Ron took a plate of brownies to a neighbor he wanted to meet. Connie took flowers to a new coworker.

If you see a new person at church, introduce yourself and offer an invitation for a cup of coffee or tea at a nearby restaurant. Make arrangements to spend time with a neighbor you don't know.

Attending a lot of functions (clubs, activities, school classes, singles' groups) provides plenty of opportunities for making casual contact. Sometimes, however, we want more than a "Hi, how are you?" We want the potential of new friendships. This too can be easy.

Stan makes it a practice to get to know one person better each week. He schedules time in his calendar to call up casual friends and acquaintances. Some weeks he just talks on the telephone. Other weeks he invites his potential friend to dinner or coffee. With this kind of investment, it's not surprising that Stan has a lot of friends.

Making these types of initial contacts, even casual ones, can be scary to people who don't feel skilled in meeting people. But it's important to remember that conversation is a skill, and skills improve with practice. If this is a problem area for you, practice these exercises:

- Go to one group function a week for the next twelve weeks.
- Initiate conversation with three people at each function.
- Try to maintain at least a five-minute conversation with each of these three people. Exchange information about your job, where you grew up, hobbies, interests, pets, or vacations.

Do these exercises faithfully, regardless of how poorly it goes, how much you don't want to, or how uncomfortable you feel. The interesting thing is that as you practice making casual contact each week, your discomfort level will decrease and your skills will increase. Also, when you know you are "practicing a skill" instead of "risking reaching out" to make a friend (and possibly being rejected), your fear level is lowered or eliminated. If someone doesn't respond to your overtures, you can tell yourself, "Oh well, I can find someone else; it's just an exercise!"

Getting Dates Isn't Necessarily the Problem

If you really wanted to, you probably could get a date for next Friday night. It may not be with the person you wanted to go out with. Or it may not be a date to the place you wanted to go to. And you may have to pay all the expenses. But you probably could get a date.

In fact, if you are feeling desperate and deprived, try this. Get a blank calendar for next month and set a goal of having three dates a day. You'll have to be creative, but it can be done. Suggestions: running before breakfast, breakfast at McDonalds, coffee break at Denny's, picnics at lunchtime, doing laundry together, concerts, dinner, plays, skating, skiing, parties, coffee and conversations, etc. Now start making calls to everyone you know and begin filling up your calendar. Oh! And you can't be too picky; just how many people would be up for a five-mile jog at five o'clock in the morning?

With some effort and commitment, you could probably fill the calendar fairly full. And the funny thing is that after a week or so, you'll be thrilled if someone calls to cancel a date! What a relief!

Frenetic activity such as this might be a welcome break for people whose social lives have been basically inactive. But most of us agree with a cartoon strip I read once. A single woman sighs because she doesn't have a date on a Friday night. She says to her friend, "If only I could have a date. Nothing serious, just a little date. Just an evening with a friend or acquaintance or even a total stranger!" The phone rings, and a man she knows asks her for a date. She tells the man she can't go on the date, saying that she has to wash her hair. After she hangs up, she says to her friend ruefully, "Apparently, I'm pickier than I thought!"

Most of us are. We don't want computer-arranged dates, stilted conversations with near strangers, or meaningless activities with people we don't like very much.

We want intimacy. We want to love and be loved. And that's the real issue!

MOVE TOWARD INTIMACY

Anyone can find people, make contact, and make dates. But it takes work to develop intimate friendships and relationships.

One of the key concepts in developing intimate friendships is not meeting fascinating people but becoming the fascinating person others want to meet. Work on these steps to becoming a more interesting person.

Become a Risk Taker

Jake has been through several bad experiences in relationships. He is almost convinced that no one will love him forever, and as a result, he approaches new relationships slowly. One can almost sense that he wears an invisible sign,

"DON'T HURT ME, PLEASE!" And feeling his insecurity, most people pass him by, unwilling either to hurt him or to discover what he's afraid of.

Jake is not a risk taker. His life is not in balance. But Jake can change that. He can take steps toward becoming ready to take risks.

The first step is to *identify areas that need work*. The second step is to *be willing to do the work*. The third step is to *do the work*.[1]

Are you cherishing fantasies that keep you from facing and dealing with reality? Identify them, release them, and remind yourself to leave them forever.

Are you facing unpleasant realities in your life? Identify what they are and make a plan to change them.

Are you facing rejection in a personal relationship? Learn not to make each encounter a total emotional risk. Don't expect each new contact to become a close, intimate friend. Instead, be friendly and let relationships develop. Risk involvement in small steps, not all at once.

Be Willing to Enjoy the Process

Joe was fishing on the wharf at dusk when a friend approached. "How's it going?"

Joe smiled, "Fine."

The friend peered at the empty creel. "Caught any fish?"

"Nope," Joe replied cheerfully.

"How long you been out here?" the friend asked.

"All day," Joe answered.

"Too bad you've wasted the whole day!" the friend sympathized.

"Oh no!" Joe explained. "I haven't wasted the day. I've been fishing!"

You see, a real fishing devotee enjoys the process. Fishing isn't just getting fish for supper. You can do that at the grocery store. But fishing is something more; it is a process some people enjoy.

In order to do well when reaching out to form new relationships, you need to learn to enjoy the process, not just be expecting the product. If Joe fished only to get fish, he would have felt the day had been wasted and might not fish that spot again. If you take classes or go to parties only to meet a possible dating partner, you'll be disappointed more often than not and you probably won't enjoy yourself in the process. Your unhappiness will communicate itself to others, and you will become unattractive to them.

Instead, enjoy the *process* of meeting new people and learning about them. If you don't become close friends, you have at least sharpened your reaching-out skills. Take classes and choose hobbies that not only will bring you in contact with interesting people but also will bring you enjoyment even if you don't meet anyone special.

Learn to enjoy risking in a new relationship, to be the first to open up, to share secrets, to commit to caring. Be real and vulnerable and enjoy the thrill of intimacy. Be the one who encourages and affirms increased openness and risking in others. Learn to enjoy each step of the process rather than just putting up with one to get to the next.

Be Patient

Good relationships take time to develop. They don't spring full blown and intimate. I'll admit that twice in my life I've met people with whom I felt an instant spark, a oneness, a closeness. Our conversations were immediately deep and intimate. It was incredible. A special gift. But most of my relationships have taken more than one meeting or conversation.

In some of my relationships the initial road was rocky. If both of us hadn't chosen to work at the relationship, we wouldn't be friends today. Relationships take work, time, energy, and patience.

Before you discard a potential friend, take a second look and try again. A friend of mine says that new friends are like a new pair of shoes. They squeak, they pinch, they look different. But if you keep wearing them a short while at a time, you'll realize one day that the leather has stretched, your foot has adjusted, and the squeak has disappeared. And you wouldn't trade the shoes for any others.

Intimacy in a relationship is a progressive process and involves several types and levels of closeness.

Recreational intimacy involves sharing leisure-time activities and interests. This is the easiest to develop because it is non-threatening and entertaining. To develop recreational intimacy, do fun things together.

Work intimacy is based on sharing mutual goals and projects, either on the job or on an extra-curricular project. This level of intimacy builds a strong bond as both people invest in a common accomplishment. To develop work intimacy, work on projects together.

Intellectual intimacy is the result of sharing ideas, thought processes, dreams, openness, and personal conclusions. People who are intellectually intimate come to know how the other person thinks and feels about things. To develop intellectual intimacy, talk with each other.

Emotional intimacy comes when people are committed to being open, honest, and caring with one another. To be emotionally intimate, risk vulnerability and commit to caring.

Conflict intimacy exists when two people are willing to work through differences in opinions, lifestyles, preferences, or desires in order to strengthen and maintain the relationship. To develop conflict intimacy, learn to confront creatively and caringly.

Spiritual intimacy is honesty about where we are in our spiritual journey. It includes sharing about our struggles, victories, prayer requests, and blessings. To be spiritually intimate, share about these things together.

Physical intimacy involves everything from a warm, bear-hug greeting to sexual intercourse. Couples who become physically intimate too soon in their relationship bypass the other levels of intimacy and often fail to build depth in the relationship. Knowing this, God gave careful rules for reserving sexual intimacy for marriage, where it could become the beautiful culmination of a full range of intimacies in a loving relationship.

TOUCH-AND-GO ENCOUNTERS

A close friend of mine was moving away, and I was angry. I had invested a lot of myself in our relationship, and I felt as if I were about to be cheated on my investment. It didn't matter that he was getting a terrific new job with travel opportunities. I wanted him to stay and be available to me.

Childish, yes. But human.

It's still hard for me to accept short-term relationships or a lessening in the level of interaction of a relationship. But people grow and change, and in the process, relationships are often redefined.

Some relationships last only for one interaction—a few hours of conversation and sharing at a conference, a chance meeting at a singles' function, or an afternoon at the park. Why the other person isn't interested in furthering the relationship may not always be known, but it's not necessarily a sign of personal rejection.

I met Bonnie at functions we both happened to attend. We always hit it off well, but neither of us pursued the friendship. Finally she called me up one day and said, "I really like you and would like to be your friend. But I think that both of us are too busy right now to take the time to develop a new relationship. My teaching semester will be over in six weeks. How about if we put each other on the back burner until then?"

Startled but intrigued, I agreed.

Six weeks later she called again. "I want off the back burner! Can we get together Saturday?"

We did and became good friends. Sometimes we need to make room in our lives for new friends.

But not everyone is ready to develop a close relationship with us at a given time. Perhaps the person is too afraid of being hurt or rejected to risk a relationship. Perhaps the person isn't aware that we would like to have a close relationship. Perhaps the person is too busy for a new relationship. Perhaps our basic interests, goals, or lifestyle is perceived as incompatible.

Instead of lamenting what we can't have, we need to enjoy what we do share. After a visit from a friend, feeling lonely, I wrote:

HE'S GONE AGAIN

Before he came,
    I dreamed a bit.

I cautioned myself.
I cleaned the house.
> And. . . . deep inside I knew each visit
> Puts a few more ghosts to sleep.

He was here.
We talked for hours.
We laughed and teased.
We touched and shared.
> And. . . . deep inside I responded to his growth
> And wished for his wisdom and skill.

He's gone again.
I feel empty.
I feel depressed.
I feel alone.
> And. . . . deep inside I know it's my choice:
> To cry because he left
> Or to smile because he came.

Is reaching out a risk? Yes. Is it worth the risk? Oh, yes! Leave loneliness behind, reach out and touch a new friend.

✔ SELF-ASSESSMENT AND FOLLOW-UP

1. How comfortable are you at reaching out? Circle the number that corresponds to your comfort level: 0 means very uncomfortable; 10 means very comfortable. Add the numbers circled to get your totals.

    0 3 6 10 I can walk up to a stranger and introduce myself.
    0 3 6 10 I can initiate and maintain interesting conversations with strangers.
    0 3 6 10 I can make the first telephone call to further a friendship.
    0 3 6 10 I can ask the other person out.
    0 3 6 10 I can let someone know I like him or her and want to get to know him or her better.
    0 3 6 10 I can say "I love you" first.
    0 3 6 10 I can share my feelings.

LEARN TO RISK

0 3 6 10 I can share my ideas.
0 3 6 10 I can share my dreams.
0 3 6 10 I can share my fears.

The total of the circled numbers is the percentage to which you are comfortable reaching out.

    0%–30%   You're almost a hermit.
    31%–50%   You're not sure you can trust people.
    51%–80%   You're fairly comfortable most of the time.
    81%–100%   You're a social person whom other people probably love to be around.

2. Resolve to make reaching out to people a priority this week.
Meet someone new.
Get to know an acquaintance better.
Be friendly to a lonely person.
Be helpful to strangers you meet.

3. Go through your Christmas-card list and write five letters to people who won't expect to hear from you.

4. Go to a singles' function and interact with at least ten people you don't know well.

5. Throw a party for your singles' group.

✔ GROUP INTERACTION

1. **Discussion.** Use the following discussion starters to get everyone involved. Work in groups of 5–10, giving each person a chance to complete the first statement before the group moves on to the next one. If a person is uncomfortable sharing, that person may pass.

    a. When I meet a person of the opposite sex, my first thought is. . . .

    b. If we start hitting it off talking together, the way I let that person know that I want to spend more time together is. . . .

    c. I think the best way to make an acquaintance into a friend is. . . .

d. One of the first problems that tends to surface when making new friends is. . . .

   e. The thing I value most in a friend is. . . . because. . . .

   f. The thing that is hardest for me to accept in a new friend is. . . .

   g. My best quality as a friend to others is. . . .

   h. An area that I'm working on to change in my relationships is. . . .

   i. When dating, my favorite activity to go out and do is. . . .

   j. What I don't like to do as a date is. . . .

2. **Cartoon Strip.** Draw a cartoon strip (using stick figures), illustrating what happens when you risk reaching out.

3. **Interview.** Play man/woman-on-the-street and interview each group member about taking the risk to reach out.

4. **Bumper Sticker.** Design bumper stickers about taking the risk to reach out. Share your designs.

9
Discover Joy

My husband, Ed, and I hurried ahead of our group to be the first to ascend to the foot of the breathtaking acropolis of Athens. Tickets in hand, we stepped inside the gates and stopped to look. I let my imagination take charge, seeing robed ancient Greeks instead of bustling tourists, admiring the splendor of the Parthenon instead of its faded ruins. I could almost hear the echo of the apostle Paul's voice from nearby Mars Hill: "Men of Athens...."

Suddenly my illusions were shattered, and reality intervened when we heard the weary voice of a tourist addressing his wife, "All right, Gertrude. I've seen it."

I turned to look for the owner of that plaintive voice. Sure enough I found him, resting on a large rock. He made it clear that he was going no further, gesturing at his wife to go on and climb to the top. He had obviously been dragged this far against his will, and he was not about to take one more step.

I meet a lot of people like that tourist. They go through life, daring anyone to prove that life is anything but pain and hard work. When they do experience something new and exciting, their basic response is, "Okay, I've seen it. So what?"

Sometimes I even find myself acting that way. When life seems like drudgery or when I feel defeated, I experience joylessness.

THE FRUIT OF THE SPIRIT IS ... JOY?

The apostle Paul tells us that the "the fruit of the Spirit is love, joy, peace, patience, kindness, goodness, faithfulness, gentleness and self-control."[1] He doesn't say that if we are filled with the Spirit, we'll develop one or even some of these characteristics. He says if we have the Holy Spirit in our lives—and as Christians the Holy Spirit lives in us—then we *have these characteristics now*. In the present!

So why do I not experience love, joy, peace . . . all of the time? I don't experience them because I've filled my life with love blockers, joy blockers, peace blockers, etc.

JOY BLOCKERS

During a seminar about dealing with pain, one man stood to share. His voice had a deadness to it as he matter-of-factly shared about his loneliness. He said that even though he was married, he felt that he was all alone. He said, unconvincingly, that he would like to feel more alive.

With gentle insight one of the leaders responded, "Sam, when you speak, I hear no emotion in your voice. But I see a lot of emotion in your eyes. What I see is sadness, deep sadness. I almost see a little boy looking wistfully into a window." The leader paused a moment before asking quietly, "Are you sad, Sam?"

Tears started rolling down Sam's cheeks as he nodded.

"How long have you been sad, Sam?" the leader asked.

Crying brokenly, Sam choked, "All of my life." And between the sobs he told his story. Of the little boy who had been abused and rejected by his father, the little boy who had always wondered what horrible thing he had done to have deserved such abuse. Of the young man who had been afraid to share himself for fear that anyone getting close would abuse and reject him again. Of the man who never let people really know him or get close enough to hurt him.

The whole group was touched by Sam's story. People cried, not just for Sam and the pain that had robbed his joy, but also for themselves and their own sadnesses as they identified with Sam.

When Sam finished his story, when he had cried out twenty-nine years of pain, the group began to respond. People shared about having similar fears. Some hugged Sam. Several thanked him for sharing. His wife, also a participant, tried to speak coherently. "Sam, all during our marriage, all I've ever wanted was to love you and be loved by you. Yet I've always felt you kept me at arms' length. Please let me in. I love you. There's nothing you could do or say to make me not love you."

Sheepishly Sam held out his arms. "I can't believe it!" he said half-laughing, half-crying, "All I ever wanted was to have someone love me, and I could have had it all along!" As they hugged, we saw Sam's face change. It had come alive. Gone was the sadness, gone the pain, replaced by a look of joy, love, and peace! A true transformation!

I'm not naïve enough to believe that Sam wouldn't need to do a lot more work in order to change a lifetime habit of holding on to his childhood pain and protecting himself from hurt. But it was incredible to see the amount of joy he found just by starting to let go and open up.

Sam didn't have to go looking for joy; joy was automatic when he got rid of his joy blocker! That's how it can be for each of us.

We all have our own ways of blocking the joy in our lives. Do any of these sound familiar?

Trying to Please Others

Jana is a people pleaser. She always asks what others want to eat before she plans a dinner. She buys little gifts for friends instead of a new dress for herself. She is so busy doing for others, no one can do for her. And what does she get for her trouble? One of her friends commented the other day, "I like Jana, but she overdoes her thoughtfulness. I wish she would just relax and be herself. She's a nice person, but she's always fussing over people!"

People-pleasing behavior usually masks a deep-seated fear that it's not okay to just be ourselves. John Powell describes this secret fear by saying that we are sometimes afraid that if we tell people who we really are, they might not like us!

The apostle Paul says it even better. "Am I now trying to win the approval of men, or of God? Or am I trying to please men? If I were still trying to please men, I would not be a servant of Christ."[2]

If we are worried about people not liking who we are,

then we're not free to become the persons God designed us to be, and our joy is blocked.

Feeling Unloved

The world is full of people waiting to love us. God. Our parents. Friends. Members of the opposite sex. Children. Old people in nursing homes. So why do we so often feel unloved?

Nathan is a good example. He has been married three times, is currently separated from his third wife, and has dated a series of women who have loved him deeply. Yet Nathan is convinced that no one will ever truly love him. He keeps sabotaging his relationships until the women finally admit defeat and let him walk away.

I've talked to several of Nathan's female friends. In each case they are more sad than angry. "Nathan may be the most loved man in history," one commented to me, "but he refuses to believe in or accept love. So he feels unloved."

I know. I dated Nathan for a while. And I loved him. But Nathan doesn't love himself. So he will never feel loved—until he accepts himself.

We have said to Nathan, "We love you, Nathan. . . ." God has said, "I love you, Nathan. . . ." But Nathan says, "Not me!" His joy is blocked.

Feeling Frustrated

Fifteen-month-old Dana was busily playing with her snap-together building pieces, laughing and pulling them until each one came apart. Finally she picked up an L-shaped piece she thought was two pieces stuck together, and she tried to unsnap it, without success. She tugged, pulled, beat it on the floor, and chewed on it, but she couldn't get it to do what she wanted it to do. She became more and more frustrated until she finally threw the piece as hard as she could and burst into tears. She was very unhappy!

We often behave like Dana when things don't go just the way we want them to go. We stubbornly insist on having things work the way we think they should work. And the end result is frustration.

My husband, Ed, dramatizes this frustration in a skit he often does for seminar groups. I tell the group that Ed's goal is to leave the room. Although the room has at least two doors Ed could use, he decides he wants to exit the room from a place in the wall where there is no door.

While we watch, Ed tries a variety of approaches to the wall. After each approach, he ends up hitting his nose on the wall.

He tries logic. "There ought to be a door here."

He asks. "I'd like a door here, please."

He begs. "Please, please, please, just for me. Be a door!"

He demands. "I must insist on a door."

He tries guilt. "After all I've done for you, painting you last spring when I'd rather have been fishing."

He becomes angry. "You ingrate! You never cared about me! If you really loved me, you'd be a door!"

He cries. "I just need a door. Nobody ever does anything special for me. Please. Just this once."

He ignores the wall and sneaks up on it, trying to catch it unawares.

As long as Ed is denying the reality that a wall is a wall is a wall, as long as he is focusing on his frustration, he can never step back and see his real options: the two doors. He will never reach his goal of leaving the room, and he will be forever frustrated and joyless.

Are there areas in which we are trying to make a wall into a door? Are we trying to force something to be something it's not?

Is it a friendship we are trying to force to be a romance?

Is it a particular promotion that we seek to the exclusion of all other options?

Is it a special ministry we want and will settle for no other?

I once met a woman who tried out for the Voices of Liberty singing group for Disney World. She was selected to be a semi-finalist. At the judging, she sang better than she had ever sung before. When they asked her (and only her) to sing the song again an octave higher, she prayed that the Holy Spirit would make her voice come out pure and sweet and not just a screech. He did. She couldn't believe that was her own voice coming out so beautifully. She knew she was going to be chosen.

But she wasn't.

For the next several weeks she didn't feel like singing at all. Her joy in singing was blocked. If she couldn't have the opportunity she wanted, she didn't want to sing again. Even when she received several requests to sing, she turned them all down.

Finally she began to acknowledge that she had two choices: she could refuse to sing and be forever unhappy, or she could sing whenever the Lord led and regain her joy in praising him. She chose to sing. Today she blesses everyone who hears her sing, and the joy of the Lord is full in her life.

Walls are walls, but praise God, there are always doors.

Feeling Out of Control

Don't you hate it when you feel as if you don't have any choice about what's happening in your life? I do! Yet we always have choices, even if we don't recognize them.

When Doreen was first a single parent, she felt tied down, even though she loved spending time with the kids. Often during those first few months she thought about the life she could have if she weren't a single parent. She listened to other women at the office, talking of parties, going shopping, or going to the movies. She felt envious and a little resentful. "I can't" was her response to most of the invitations offered, "I've got to stay home with the kids."

Summer came. The children went to spend eight weeks with their father, and Doreen learned a surprising truth. Her life was no different from before. She accepted very few invitations to go to parties, shopping, or the movies.

She finally realized that single parenting was not the real reason she had refused the earlier invitations. She had said no because she didn't enjoy those things! When the children returned, they found a more joyful, less resentful mom!

Sometimes we don't have control over what happens in our lives, but we always have a choice about how we respond to what occurs.

STEPS TO JOY

Whether joy is blocked in our lives by the pain of trying to please others, by feeling unloved, frustrated, or out of control, we can find the joy by letting go of the pain and choosing to remove the joy blockers.

Do Right

A counselor asked Michael, "What is something you do right even when you don't want to?"

Mike had to think a while about the question. Finally he thought of an answer and told the counselor.

"And how do you feel when you know you're doing the right thing?" the counselor asked.

Mike's face brightened. "I feel real good," he admitted with a big smile.

It's true. It feels real good to do what's right—to eat right, to exercise, to be kind when you would rather return evil for evil.

A neighbor's boy had written all over my front door with indelible ink. I tried everything, but I couldn't get it off. Finally I wrote a note to the neighbor, asking that she fix my door. I left out all of the nasty thoughts I had about her little son and kept to the facts.

Her response was one of the meanest and nastiest letters I've ever read. She called me names, blamed my son for every bad thing that had happened on the street, and on and on. I was furious! I could hardly work the next day because my mind was full of turmoil. At first I started thinking of what I could say to her in my next letter, knowing full well I wouldn't write the words. Yet I felt I had to do something.

Suddenly I had an idea. I remembered the words of Romans 12:18–21. "If it is possible, as far as it depends on you, live at peace with everyone. Do not take revenge, my friends, but leave room for God's wrath, for it is written, 'It is mine to avenge; I will repay,' says the Lord. On the contrary: 'If your enemy is hungry, feed him; if he is thirsty, give him something to drink. In doing this, you will heap burning coals on his head.' Do not be overcome by evil, but overcome evil with good."

I picked up the phone and ordered flowers to be sent to my neighbor. It was the best $20 I ever spent. Immediately I felt a little giggle start inside. My only regret was that I wouldn't be there to see the look of shock when she read the card and saw that the flowers were from me. Can you just imagine? My neighbor was still on my mind most of the day, but instead of grinding my teeth, I found myself smiling as I pictured her receiving my flowers.

That night her husband came over and painted my door. But by then the door wasn't actually important. The lesson I had learned was more significant to me.

Try it sometime, I guarantee you'll find it surprisingly fun! Send flowers to someone who has wronged you. FTD florists could have a whole new slogan: "Feel good! Send flowers to the one you don't feel like loving!"

Doing right feels great! When I refuse to give in to temptation or to respond angrily to a hostile person, I feel great. And those times when I don't do right, I can still make it right by repenting and confessing to God. Then I feel joy again. King David, after repenting of his sin with Bathsheba, prayed that God would restore the joy he had felt before his adulterous relationship.[3]

Set aside time to be alone and consider areas in which you need to clean up your lifestyle and get back on the right track. Clear up your conscience before God and vow to do right in his strength.

Joy will begin to flow.

Be Real

Real people are those who let you get to know them as they are, without pretense or apologies. Real people know that none of us is perfect but that all of us are growing and improving as best we can. Real people don't expect everyone else to like them but are generally well liked just because they are real.

My favorite people are real people. One of them is Lou. He is kind, considerate, and open-minded. He doesn't put on airs or pretend to be someone he is not. While he hasn't put in a lot of time in classrooms, his life experience has gained him more knowledge and practical wisdom than most college graduates I know. Lou says what he thinks and doesn't always agree with instructions from his boss. But he gets the job done and done right.

LEARN TO RISK

Lou used to work for me, and I miss him now. He was more than an employee; he was my friend. He was real.

Learning to be real with others comes after many risks, many failures, many small successes. In the children's book *The Velveteen Rabbit*, Margery Williams says some powerful things about the process.

> "Does it hurt?" asked the Rabbit.
> "Sometimes," said the Skin Horse, for he was always truthful. "When you are Real you don't mind being hurt."
> "Does it happen all at once, like being wound up," he asked, "or bit by bit?"
> "It doesn't happen all at once," said the Skin Horse. "You become. It takes a long time. That's why it doesn't often happen to people who break easily, or have sharp edges, or who have to be carefully kept. Generally, by the time you are Real, most of your hair has been loved off, and your eyes drop out and you get loose in the joints and very shabby. But these things don't matter at all, because once you are Real you can't be ugly, except to people who don't understand."
> The Rabbit sighed. He thought it would be a long time before this magic called Real happened to him. He longed to become Real, to know what it felt like; and yet the idea of growing shabby and losing his eyes and whiskers was rather sad. He wished that he could become it without these uncomfortable things happening to him."[4]

When we can be ourselves, when we don't have to pretend, we can toss away the masks, the lists of secrets, the fears, and just *be*. As a result, joy begins to spring up.

Be Curious and Creative

Abe went to an afternoon art class and two hours later emerged with a completed landscape. He had never before tried oil painting, yet here was evidence that with training, he could probably paint beautiful pictures. He had never before considered painting as a creative outlet, but every time he looked at his landscape, he felt excited.

Be like Abe—try new things. Allow your creativity to surface and blossom. Become curious and discover different ways to express yourself. Art. Music. Writing. Hobbies. Sports. What new avenues can you find to try?

Creativity can also serve as an important outlet. When we feel strong negative emotions, our bodies prepare themselves physiologically either to run or fight. They produce an excess of physical energy. We can choose to use that energy either positively or negatively.

When Betty is upset, she takes out her quilt and begins to work quietly. Inevitably she finds herself intrigued, and her frustration, anger, or irritation begins to fade. Hank works on his car for the same kind of "therapy." Sandra bakes. Val cleans closets.

We can be creative in other ways. The Bible tells us that each of us has been given a spiritual gift.[5] When we discover our gifts and use them, we begin to sense the higher purpose for our lives and find incredible fulfillment.

Take time to appreciate God's creativity. See his handiwork in the clouds, sunrises, sunsets, trees, flowers, mountains, and the sea and surf.

On one of my trips to Florida, I arrived late in the evening, tired from traveling. The woman who met me at the airport casually mentioned that we were only a half a mile from the ocean. Suddenly revived, I said, "The ocean?"

Quickly picking up my interest, the woman said, "Do you want to?" I nodded. We went down and walked barefoot in the sand under the stars. It was wonderfully restorative.

When I take time to examine what God creates, when I exercise creativity, I find joy is inevitable.

Share Your Life with Others

The candlelight dinner had been perfect. The food, the conversation, the table setting, the music were just wonderful. Then came the best part. Dale reached for Marti's hand, looked deeply into her eyes, and asked her to marry him. He handed her a single white rosebud and told her to look inside. Nestled deep inside the flower was a beautiful engagement ring. The moment was magic.

As much as Marti loved what was happening, she was already anticipating the fun of telling and retelling this story to her friends and family. There's joy in sharing.

A poster says it well: Friends divide grief and multiply joy. How true.

Sharing, caring, and loving are joyful ways to live. We won't find a lot of joy if we sit alone in our living rooms and don't communicate with anybody.

We need to share our lives with each other. It keeps our feet on the ground. It provides perspective, feedback, and encouragement. And when our fellowship is with Christians, we can experience an even deeper level of support and love. When we communicate and share with one another, joy comes to our lives. It's a little difficult to maintain an abundant supply of ever-bubbling joy if we don't interact with others. When we communicate, share, and care, we feel alive.

When something exciting happens to us, what is the first thing we often do? We tell somebody. Or we phone a friend, coworker, or relative. Communicating is an essential part of joy. And the Bible encourages us to share not only with other people but also with the Lord himself.[6]

The Bible says that Christ endured the Cross and its shame because of the *joy* that was set before him.[7] What was the joy that was set before him? I believe it is the joy of having us eternally communicating, relating, glorifying, praising, and sharing with him. And I ask myself, am I giving him that kind of joy? He endured the Cross for me, not just to save me, but to have joy. Am I giving him back that joy?

We need to relate to the Lord. And we need to relate to other people. When we do, we find joy.

Serve

Charles is a helper. He loves to assist people in need. Whether it's giving information, showing them how, or running errands, he loves to do it.

Ellen had been a secretary for fifteen years when she got a boss who saw her potential. He began to encourage her, and within a few months she had gone from, "You must be kidding" to "I'll give it a try!" Two weeks later she applied for a promotion and got it. Ellen gave her boss a card he still treasures. On the front is a turtle and the word "Thanks." Inside it reads: "for bringing me out of my shell!" Ellen's boss served her through his encouragement.

The joy of helping is discovering that it's often much more blessed to give than to receive!

Abide in the Lord

Joy comes not only when we actively do things but also when we learn to rest in the Lord. What does it mean to rest in the Lord, to abide in him? John's gospel uses the image of a grapevine to explain that each of us is like a branch of the vine: we gain our life-giving nutrients from the trunk of the vine—Jesus Christ.[8] As long as we stay closely connected to the Lord and receive our nourishment from him, we will find joy.

In the first few verses of John 15, we learn that joy comes

After we are real (v. 2)

After we do right (v. 4)

After we are productive (v. 5)

After we fellowship (v. 7).

When we abide in Christ and his words abide in us, we find love and joy: "Just as the Father has loved Me, I have also loved you; abide in My love. If you keep My commandments, you will abide in My love; just as I have kept My Father's commandments, and abide in his love. These things I have spoken to you, that My joy may be in you, and that your joy may be made full."[9] Not that we'll get a little capsule dose everyday and have to say, "Oh, please, may I have more joy? I'm just about out." The verse says our joy will be full, complete, lacking nothing. What a promise!

Give Thanks

When we thank people, we experience joy. When we appreciate what other people have done for us and when we take the time to say thank you, we feel joy. When I write a thank-you note and say, "Every time I use that oak trivet you gave me, I think of you. I have enjoyed it so much," I feel joyful.

Joy springs up when we give thanks, when we really count our blessings, when we praise God for what he is doing. Many Scripture verses promise us joy. They range from "weeping may endure for a night, but joy comes in the morning" to "the joy of the Lord is my strength."[10] One of my favorites is the exuberant benediction found at the end of the book of Jude: "Now unto him that is able to keep you from falling, and to present you faultless before the presence of his glory with exceeding joy." I like that last phrase "with exceeding joy." We are not going to march up to heaven and say to God, "Well, I did it; I hope you're proud. I hope you're satisfied. I suffered for you all my life, and I just want you to know I did it. I'm glad I made it into heaven." No, the verse promises that he will present us before the presence of his glory with exceeding joy.

We needn't wait for eternity to start giving him that joy! We can start now!

✔ SELF-ASSESSMENT AND FOLLOW-UP

1. Place an X on the line to represent your level of joy in each of the following areas:

Joyless   So-so   Joyful

_____ Work

_____ Leisure activities

_____ Church activities

_____ School

_____ Same-sex friendships

_____ Opposite-sex friendships

_____ Relationship to dating partner

_____ Relationships to parents

_____ Relationships to siblings

_____ Relationships to children

_____ Self-discipline

_____ Exercise patterns

_____ Diet

_____ Control of your temper

_____ Coping strengths

_____ Hobbies

_____ Home making

_____ Decision making

DISCOVER JOY

Joyless   So-so   Joyful
_____ Choices

How joyful are you? Do you experience a lack of joy in significant areas of your life? If so, for how long has this been true? What are you going to do about this?

2. Write a letter to a friend, sharing about a joyful experience you've had.

3. List at least ten things, relationships, or activities that make you happy.

4. Define happiness without using words like *joy*, *contentment*, *gladness*, *peace*, *satisfaction*, *pleasure*, *cheerfulness*.

5. Reflect on what prevents you from being happy. In your journal, set three goals for overcoming these obstacles. Check on your progress in a week.

✓ GROUP INTERACTION

1. **Discussion.** Use the following discussion starters to get everyone involved. Work in groups of 5–10, giving each person a chance to respond to the first statement before the group moves on to the next one. If a person is uncomfortable sharing, that person may pass.

   a. When do you find it difficult to be joyful?

   b. What are the scriptural reasons for joy?

   c. What is God saying to you about the level of joy in your life?

   d. Share about a time when you "lost your resolve" to do right because of a relationship.

   e. Share about a time when you "lost your perspective" in a relationship.

   f. Share about a time when you "lost your strength" in a relationship.

   g. Share about a relationship that kept you from the abundant life.

h. Share about a relationship that encourages you to stand firm.

i. Share about a friendship that gives you strength.

j. Share about a friendship that enriches your life and encourages you to live the abundant life.

2. **Scripture Search.** Read the following Scripture verses and jot down key ideas about joy expressed in each one. Then share with the group one or two verses that speak to your present situation.

Psalm 16:11	John 15:11
Psalm 30:5	John 16:20–22
Psalm 32:11	John 17:13
Psalm 43:4	Galatians 5:22
Psalm 51:12	1 Thessalonians 2:19
Psalm 126:5	James 1:2
Proverbs 23:24	1 Peter 1:8
Luke 15:7	1 Peter 4:13
John 3:29	1 John 1:4

3. **Poem.** Write a short poem expressing your joy. Share your poems with one another.

4. **Picture.** Draw a picture of joy with everyone in the group contributing to it.

5. **Pantomime.** Pantomime a joyous experience you once had.

10
Celebrate Life

Have you ever had a day when there seemed to be nothing to celebrate? One of those days when life is either dull and boring or full of problems and obstacles?

You wake up late because your alarm didn't ring. When you finally get to your office, you realize you've got a spot of grease on your suit. Your boss wants a project you haven't finished, the typist calls in sick, and the copy machine doesn't work.

You spend your lunch hour waiting at the restaurant where your friend said she would meet you, only to realize after half an hour that you had agreed to meet the *next* day.

On the way home from work you run out of gas and wait alongside the highway for forty-five minutes before you get help. Then as you turn the corner to your own street, you spot a bumper sticker that says, "Smile! Have a nice day!" You suddenly have this overwhelming urge to ram your car into that bumper and see if the other driver smiles.

We've all had times like that—times when celebrating life is the last thing we feel ready to do. And yet some people seem to celebrate each new experience, even each disaster.

Leilani is one of those people. I love to visit her, just to hear her stories. I used to think that Leilani lived a more adventurous life than most people, but then I realized that it wasn't her experiences that were so interesting, it was her *attitude* about her experiences. She finds humor in almost any situation. When she recounts a frustrating experience, she makes it sound like a television comedy routine. By the time she finishes her story, both she and I have laughed until our sides ache.

I decided to become like Leilani. Instead of getting depressed and playing "poor me," I now try to find the humor in what happens to me. It's amazing what a difference a change of attitude can make. Remember the old saying, "It's not what happens to you that matters, but how you respond to what happens."

A couple of years ago my husband and I planned a trip to Egypt. We prepared ourselves for our trip not only by buying proper clothing but also by mentally preparing ourselves for the heat and the hours of walking we would do.

About a month before our trip we had an experience that taught us something about our attitudes. We needed to stop at the grocery store, but when we drove in the parking lot, we couldn't find an empty spot anywhere. We had to park two blocks away! I was irritated. As we walked from the car, I fussed and fumed. Ed finally suggested, "Let's just say we're practicing for Egypt!" We laughed, linked hands, and energetically walked the entire distance, smiling all the way. From then on "practicing for Egypt" became our password for accepting problems, letting go of anger, and retaining a positive attitude. I'll admit that sometimes I can't imagine Egypt being this bad! But the reality is that our attitudes are the basis for whether or not we live in a celebration mode.

TODAY WAS MADE FOR JOY

Sounds of laughter float into my study from the children playing outside my window. They make happy, carefree, intensely energetic now sounds. I watch in wonder.

Have you laughed today? This week? Just how often do you find yourself laughing out of the pure enjoyment of being alive? Sometimes we find ourselves so busy with an overloaded schedule that the sound of our own laughter is foreign to our ears!

At other times we can laugh at embarrassments and problems. I remember one of those times. A friend received a call during her dinner hour from a bill collector who proceeded not only to demand his money but also to criticize her character, person, financial responsibility, and her fitness to be considered a worthwhile human being.

During the call my friend struggled to control her temper as she explained her side of the story and made arrangements to make the payment. Then she hung up. Visibly shaken, she pushed aside her plate and expressed her anger at the caller. She wanted to get back at him for his rudeness. We began to fantasize about all the outrageous ways to let the collector know how his telephone manner made my friend feel.

Within minutes we were laughing merrily at our own silliness. The situation had changed from an angry frustration to an opportunity for some much-needed humor. "I've never in my life laughed so much over a bill collector's call!" my friend sighed, wiping the tears from her eyes.

What makes us able to see the lighter side of life? The secret is a deep, inner confidence that we will get through our difficult times as long as we don't take ourselves or the world too seriously.

As the song reminds us—take the time to smell the roses—today! We can relax. We can take a few deep breaths and become aware of our position in the world.

Look down. We'll always find people whose problems are worse than ours. The forgotten. The deserted. The beaten. The dying.

Look around. Others share problems and limitations similar to ours. We can find a supportive community if we reach out to the right people.

Look up. God is always with us. He loves us. He cares. He can see the future. He knows how all this is going to come out! Trust him!

How can we lose? Today is the day the Lord made. Let's celebrate it.[1]

I CAN'T CELEBRATE BECAUSE. . . .

Nick has an attitude problem. Underlying his whole approach to life is a basic anger at God, life in general, and all women. Even when he's being pleasant, his anger is just below the surface. His temper is quick and easily provoked. Nick says he wants to change, but he won't let go of his anger.

Many people are like Nick. They are crippled by negative attitudes, and their lives are devoid of any joy or celebration.

Psychologist Albert Ellis describes eleven irrational beliefs that can rob a person of joy.[2]

1. Everyone Should Love Us

We don't consciously hold this belief because we know that not everyone is going to like us, let alone love us! But very often we demonstrate by our actions that deep inside, we believe everyone should love us.

Darlene can't take criticism from anyone, even people whose opinions she doesn't value. She becomes depressed and defensive. She feels that criticism means the person doesn't like/love/approve of her.

Daryl can't say no to any request or invitation. He's afraid the other person might be offended and not like him.

Patti is always giving gifts, sending cards, bringing flowers, and doing favors. Sometimes she does these things even when she doesn't feel like it. She wants to be loved and accepted by everyone, all of the time.

Darlene, Daryl, and Patti live in bondage, in an irrational fear of not being loved. They work at pleasing people. As a result, they're not always genuine and real.

A more rational approach is to be true to our own standards and to work at self-improvement. When we encounter criticism, disapproval, or even rejection, we can look at the situation and analyze the issues. If we need to make a personal change, then we can work toward that goal. If the issue is one of personal preference, then we can acknowledge the difference and not be devastated by it.

2. We Should Be Perfect

We all know that nobody's perfect, yet much of the time we act on the irrational belief that we should be! Dale has never admitted to being wrong or apologized for something he said or did. Sharyl is so afraid of appearing foolish that she won't try a new skill or take part in something new. Kate is devastated and overly apologetic if she forgets something or makes a mistake.

We all want to do our best, but if we live in constant fear of failing, we make life a chore rather than a celebration.

3. We Have No Control over Our Happiness

People who operate from this irrational belief let happenings control their happiness (or, in most cases, their lack of it). They depend on others to "make their day," to dispel their loneliness, and to point out the flowers along the way.

"I get depressed every Christmas," Art confesses. "I hate holidays. Everyone is busy with their families and plans. I feel so left out." Art sees himself as a helpless victim of his circumstances.

Not Betsy. Knowing she would miss her kids (who go to their father's house for holidays), she starts planning early to make the holidays special. One year she went to London for Christmas. While there, she attended the Christmas Eve service at Westminster Abbey and sang Christmas carols on the steps of St. Martin-in-the-Fields Church at Trafalgar Square. Another year she planned a "movie safari" and saw all of the new Christmas-release films by going to two a day for a week. One year she went to Mexico. Still another she had an old-fashioned house party with taffy pulling, tree trimming, table games, and Christmas caroling. Betsy's coworkers can't wait to hear what she has planned for this year!

4. We Can't Change the Influence of Our Past

Bob's favorite expression to excuse any fault is, "I was raised that way." Whether it's for his chronic lateness or his insensitivity, Bob's excuse says, "I can't change the way I am."

While we are influenced by our past experiences, we need not be ruled by those experiences. We can *choose to change.*

When I was six years old, I persistently begged for something until I got it. But then I felt awful because I knew that my begging had made the giver angry. I decided then that I would never ask for anything again. Over twenty years later I became aware that this irrational belief had created problems in my relationships. Not only did I not make legitimate requests of others, but I also was not a good receiver when somebody voluntarily gave me something. I had to choose to change my patterns of thinking and behaving.

The point is that we can make personal changes. We are who we are by choice. And the difference between who we are and who we become, is what we do.

5. Every Problem Has One Perfect Solution

Elise doesn't get along with her boss. She recognizes they have problems, but she hasn't done anything about it because she is waiting for the perfect solution. Each day she comes home frustrated and angry about how he treats her.

But Elise's good friend Claudia has been a big help. Once a week Claudia and Elise get together for dinner at a restaurant. For the first several weeks, Claudia just listened to Elise's complaints. Then she began to ask Elise, "What do you think you can do about it?"

Elise's typical response was, "Nothing will ever change him."

But as the weeks progressed, Claudia patiently helped Elise talk through a set of alternatives to her problem. At first they only talked about the alternatives because Elise was sure none of them would work. They listed the advantages and disadvantages of each approach. This exercise was new for Elise, who before had looked only at the disadvantages of possible solutions. Then Claudia encouraged Elise to choose a solution that most appealed to her, even if it wasn't the perfect solution. After Elise tried the approach, she and Claudia discussed how it had worked. If the approach hadn't work well, Claudia encouraged Elise to continue to try different approaches until she found one that was effective.

Through the patient efforts of her friend, Elise learned not only that she had many alternatives to approach the problem with her boss but also that she had alternatives to other problem areas in her life. Once she abandoned her irrational belief of trying to find the perfect solution, she was able to move beyond several of her ruts.

6. We Should Expect the Worst

Jill jokes about Murphy's Law, "If something can go wrong, it will." Harriet lives by it. She firmly believes that every cloud has a black lining, that every gift is a Trojan horse. While she acknowledges that some good things do happen, she pays little attention to them and dwells instead on the bad.

If we look for the bad, we can find it. If we expect the worst, it may occur. But even if it doesn't, we have wasted our life expecting it to!

Sure, bad things do happen, even to people with positive attitudes. But anticipating bad things by worrying or fretting doesn't help. And the truth is that when bad things do happen, most of us find the strength to cope! We need to leave behind our irrational fears and get on with life.

7. Someone Should Take Care of Us

Isn't it strange how the teenager who rebels at being taken care of by parents can grow up to be an adult who is looking for a caretaker? Will is very dependent. He hates being single, not because he is lonely but because he has no one to do his laundry, cook his meals, mend his clothes, or clean his apartment. Fanny wants a man to take the responsibility for her car repairs, her lawn, and her teenaged son.

The dependent person is at the mercy of the person he or she leans on. Rational adults want to make their own decisions and take charge of their own lives.

8. It's Catastrophic If Our Plans Fall Through

The English poet Robert Burns reminds us that the best laid schemes of mice and men often go awry. Still we forget!

Kelly is a very organized person. When out-of-town guests come to visit her, she is prepared with a packaged tour. One-day guests get a walking tour of the major historical sites in Old Town and dinner at a famous fish restaurant. Two-day guests get the above, plus a trip to the wild animal park, a picnic lunch, and a play, concert, or movie. She has a complete schedule for visits of up to one week. Which is terrific.

Except when a guest doesn't want to go to the zoo or have fish for dinner. Then Kelly's day is ruined! She's not very flexible.

Gerard isn't like Kelly, but he has a problem with this same irrational belief. He always wanted to be a veterinarian.

He studied hard, made good grades, and then couldn't get into any veterinary schools for five years because of the waiting lists. He was devastated! Instead of making alternate plans for a career while he waited, he dropped out of life, quit work, and basically spent five unhappy years waiting for his goal. Eventually he did become a veterinarian, but he was bitter for years at having had to wait.

By all means make plans. But don't expect them to work out exactly as you want them to and don't let the obstacles rob you of the joy of living.

9. It's Better to Avoid Tough Realities Than to Face Them

Peter spends twice as much energy getting out of doing something than it would take to just get up and do the job. Do you know people like that?

Procrastinating and avoiding reality are terrific energy sappers. Unfinished projects not only clutter up our homes, but they also take up emotional and psychological space in our lives.

When Tricia feels overwhelmed by having too much to do, she makes a list. Then instead of concentrating on doing the big, time-consuming projects, she takes a whole day and tackles fifteen to twenty of the small, annoying items. She claims that her energy level increases each time she crosses something off the list. Because of her renewed energy, she usually finishes the bigger projects in shorter time than usual.

When Theo is afraid to do something, his approach is to do it instead of stewing about it. "It works," he claims. "If I just go ahead and confront that friend or attempt that project, I feel much better about myself than if I hold back and give in to fear."

10. Bad People Should Be Punished

Denise lives out this irrational belief so completely that she thinks anyone who doesn't measure up to her standards should be punished too! If someone doesn't recognize a character flaw in himself or herself, Denise feels compelled to point it out. If someone behaves thoughtlessly or unfeelingly, Denise tells the person off. If someone lets her down, Denise is unforgiving and ruthless. Her blood pressure rises when she reads the news, and she is forever fighting for a "cause."

Denise needs to let people be where they are and allow them their faults. She needs to learn to forgive. And she needs to learn that it's God's responsibility, not hers, to judge others' behavior.[3]

11. We Must Get Upset over Our Friend's Problems

People who operate from this irrational belief often create more problems than they solve. When I told my friend Meredith that someone had slighted me and hurt my feelings, she became more angry than I had been. She sometimes would even go to straighten out the offender.

That's not what I needed from a friend. What I needed was someone to listen to my story, encourage and affirm me, and then let me solve my own problems. Finally I shared this with Meredith, who agreed to try the new approach. It worked well! She no longer felt compelled to take on all my problems, and I was free to share things without fearing that she would interfere.

We need to care for one another, even to weep together, but we must not become steamrollers who try to level other people's lives for them.

A NEW START

Jesus said he came to earth so that we could live an abundant, full life.[4] Is your life full? Free? Abundant? If not, now is the time to make a new start.

Reset your goals. Identify areas that you want to develop. What do you want to become or experience? What do you want to learn or acquire or know? Set a goal about one or more of these areas. Then break down the goal into measurable and reachable steps. Finally, set a time when you would like to see that goal accomplished.

Renew the commitment. Commit yourself to reaching your goals. Vow to devote the required time, energy, and effort to doing what you have set out to accomplish. Acknowledge that you temporarily may have to set aside some activities in order to meet your objectives.

Rethink the process. What is it going to take to become a person who lives each day to the fullest, not just cramming each moment with action? What will it take for you to develop healthful attitudes toward life? What will it take to

- take healthy risks
- let go of the past
- forgive other people and yourself
- release fear
- accept reality
- risk reaching out
- relax and view life as a celebration?

Regain the victory. Robert Fulghum wrote,

> All I ever really needed to know I learned in kindergarten.
>
> Most of what I really need to know about how to live and what to do and how to be, I learned in kindergarten. Wisdom was not at the top of the graduate school mountain, but there in the sandbox at nursery school.
>
> These are the things I learned: Share everything. Play fair. Don't hit people. Put things back where you found them. Clean up your own mess. Don't take things that aren't yours. Say you're sorry when you hurt somebody. Wash your hands before you eat. Flush. Warm cookies and cold milk are good for you. Live a balanced life. Learn some and think some and draw and paint and sing and dance and play and work every day some.
>
> Take a nap every afternoon. When you go out into traffic, hold hands and stick together. Be aware of wonder. Remember the little seeds in the plastic cup. The roots go down and the plant grows and nobody really knows how or why, but we are all like that.
>
> Goldfish and hamsters and white mice and even little seeds in the plastic cup—they all die. So do we.
>
> And then remember the book about Dick and Jane and the first word you learned, the biggest word of all: LOOK. Everything you need to know is in there somewhere. The Golden Rule and love and basic sanitation. Ecology and politics and sane living.
>
> Think of what a better world it would be if we all—the whole world—had cookies and milk about 3 o'clock every afternoon and then lay down with our blankets for a nap. Or if we had a basic policy in our nation and other nations

to always put things back where we found them and cleaned up our own messes. And it is still true, no matter how old you are, when you go out into the world, it is best to hold hands and stick together.[5]

Life is difficult. But you can be a victor rather than a victim! Take charge. Choose to be happy. Celebrate life!

✔ SELF-ASSESSMENT AND FOLLOW-UP

1. Place an X in front of each irrational belief that is a problem for you.

    ___ Everyone should love me.

    ___ I should be perfect.

    ___ I have no control over my happiness.

    ___ I can't change the influence of my past.

    ___ Every problem has one perfect solution.

    ___ I should expect the worst.

    ___ Someone should take care of me.

    ___ It's catastrophic if my plans fall through.

    ___ It's better to avoid tough realities than to face them.

    ___ Bad people should be punished.

    ___ I must be very upset over my friend's problems.

    What can you do to begin rethinking these beliefs and start facing reality more frequently?

2. List the ways you celebrated life this week.

3. Plan a mini-celebration each day this week to rejoice over a positive aspect of your life.

4. Plan a celebration party. On the invitations tell each person to come prepared to celebrate something special. Decorate with red, yellow, and orange colors. Bake "smile" cookies.

5. List in your journal the blessings God has given you this week. Pray, thanking him for his goodness.

LEARN TO RISK

✔ GROUP INTERACTION

1. **Discussion.** Use the following discussion starters to get everyone involved in the discussion. Work in groups of 5–10, giving each person a chance to respond to the first statement before the group moves on to the next one. If a person is uncomfortable sharing, that person may pass.

   a. How did you celebrate life today?

   b. How could you have celebrated today?

   c. What makes life a celebration for you?

   d. What keeps you from celebrating now?

   e. Share about a time (or experience) when you celebrated life.

   f. What person in your acquaintance celebrates life well?

   g. In what ways would you like to be like that person?

   i. What is the hardest thing to celebrate?

2. **Graph.** Draw a pie graph to represent how you spend your time. (example: 35% working, 20% sleeping, 10% church activities, 10% friendships, 5% eating, 5% fun, 5% personal devotions, 10% with your children, if you have any). Shade the areas to indicate the degree to which that area is satisfying to you right now: use light shading to indicate little satisfaction, dark shading to indicate great satisfaction.

   a. Which areas are the least satisfying?

   b. How long have those areas been so unsatisfying?

   c. How do you contribute to keeping them unsatisfying?

   d. What have you done to improve those areas?

   e. What can you do to make your life more abundant in these areas?

3. **Advertising brochure.** Design an advertising brochure for a joyful life. Share it with the rest of the group.

4. **Jingle.** Write a jingle about celebrating life. Sing it for each other.

Notes

INTRODUCTION
1. Jesus tells us that he came to earth so that we "may have and enjoy life, and have it in abundance—to the full, till it overflows" (John 10:10b AMPLIFIED).
2. Philippians 3:13–14.
3. Psalm 118:24.

CHAPTER 1
1. Bob Getz, "Do You, Knight in Shining Armor, Take This Woman?" *Eagle Beacon* (Wichita, Kansas), August 1, 1985.
2. 1 Samuel 25:2–42.
3. Ruth 3:1–4:13.
4. Genesis 2:18–23.
5. Genesis 24.
6. 1 Kings 3:5–14.
7. 2 Kings 20:1–6.
8. Genesis 41:14–46.
9. 1 Samuel 1:5–20.
10. Matthew 14:22–33.
11. Acts 16:25–26.
12. Matthew 6:28–34, James 4:13–15, and Proverbs 27:1 encourage us to live fully each present day.
13. Proverbs 13:12 NASB.
14. Romans 13:8a NASB.

CHAPTER 2
1. Proverbs 18:13 TLB.
2. Ephesians 1:6 KJV reminds us that we are "accepted in the beloved" by God.
3. Galatians 4:16.
4. 1 Corinthians 13:4–5.

5. Ephesians 4:15.
6. Galatians 5:1.
7. Emily Coleman, *Brief Encounters* (New York: Doubleday, 1979).
8. In Philippians 4:8–9, Paul says we are not to dwell on unpleasant, unproductive thoughts, but to concentrate on what is pure, good, true, just, and profitable.
9. Galatians 5:22–23 reminds us that if we allow the Holy Spirit to rule our lives, we will reflect these godly characteristics: love, joy, peace, patience, kindness, goodness, faithfulness, gentleness, and self-control.
10. Jeremiah 29:11.
11. Romans 8:28.
12. Philippians 1:6.
13. John 6:37.

CHAPTER 3

1. Job 29:2–7a TLB.
2. Genesis 19:15–26.
3. Luke 17:28–33.
4. Paraphrase of Philippians 3:13–14.
5. Ephesians 4:31.
6. Hebrews 12:1 TLB.
7. Isaiah 43:18–19a.
8. Matthew 7:7–9.
9. James 4:2–3.
10. Isaiah 43:2.
11. Isaiah 61:3 TLB.
12. Psalm 126:5 TLB.
13. Ezra 3.

CHAPTER 4

1. Matthew 6:34b.
2. See Matthew 6:12.
3. Ephesians 4:26–27, 31–32 PHILLIPS.
4. Genesis 37:2–47:26.
5. Genesis 41:51.
6. Psalm 103:3a, emphasis added.
7. Matthew 6:14–15.
8. 1 John 1:9.

CHAPTER 5

1. Deuteronomy 34:7–12.
2. Joshua 1:2.
3. Joshua 1:9.
4. 1 Peter 5:7.
5. Jeremiah 29:11.

NOTES

6. 1 Corinthians 2:9 NASB.
7. Psalm 118:24 TLB.
8. 1 Corinthians 13:1–3.

CHAPTER 6

1. John 10:10.
2. Jeremiah 29:11.
3. Romans 12:2; 1 Corinthians 2:9.
4. 1 Samuel 16:1; 2 Samuel 2:4.
5. The sermon was preached by Pastor Charles Crabtree at Bethel Church, San Jose, California.
6. Paraphrase of 1 Samuel 16:7b.
7. Romans 8:29.
8. John 15:14, 17; John 13:34.
9. John 14:16.
10. Zig Ziglar, *See You at the Top* (Pelican, 1984), 113–114.
11. Isaiah 40:29–31.
12. Galatians 6:9 TLB.

CHAPTER 7

1. Galatians 6:7–8.
2. Jim Rohn is an internationally known entrepreneur and business consultant. His seminar was called "The Making of a Leader."
3. Luke 6:38 TLB.
4. Deuteronomy 33:25b.
5. See John 9:4; Ephesians 5:14–17.
6. See 1 Peter 5:8.
7. Mark 4:3–20.

CHAPTER 8

1. James 1:22–25 reminds us that it's not enough to listen to God's instructions; we must obey them. We must take the initiative and do it.

CHAPTER 9

1. Galatians 5:22–23a.
2. Galatians 1:10.
3. Psalm 51:12.
4. Margery Williams, *The Velveteen Rabbit* (New York: Simon and Schuster, 1983).
5. 1 Corinthians 12.
6. 1 John 1:6–7.
7. Hebrews 12:2.
8. John 15:1–11.
9. John 15:9–11 NASB.

10. Nehemiah 8:10b and Psalm 30:5b NKJV.

CHAPTER 10
1. Paraphrase of Psalm 118:24.
2. John Powell, *Fully Human, Fully Alive* (Argus Communications, 1976), 118–20.
3. Romans 12:19.
4. John 10:10.
5. Robert Fulghum, *All I Really Needed to Know I Learned in Kindergarten* (New York: Random House, 1988), reprinted by permission from *Church and Public Education*.